CW00801380

MariaDB Essentials

Quickly get up to speed with MariaDB, the leading,
drop-in replacement for MySQL, through this
practical tutorial

Emilien Kenler

Federico Razzoli

[PACKT] open source
PUBLISHING community experience distilled

BIRMINGHAM - MUMBAI

MariaDB Essentials

Copyright © 2015 Packt Publishing

All rights reserved. No part of this book may be reproduced, stored in a retrieval system, or transmitted in any form or by any means, without the prior written permission of the publisher, except in the case of brief quotations embedded in critical articles or reviews.

Every effort has been made in the preparation of this book to ensure the accuracy of the information presented. However, the information contained in this book is sold without warranty, either express or implied. Neither the authors, nor Packt Publishing, and its dealers and distributors will be held liable for any damages caused or alleged to be caused directly or indirectly by this book.

Packt Publishing has endeavored to provide trademark information about all of the companies and products mentioned in this book by the appropriate use of capitals. However, Packt Publishing cannot guarantee the accuracy of this information.

First published: October 2015

Production reference: 1231015

Published by Packt Publishing Ltd.
Livery Place
35 Livery Street
Birmingham B3 2PB, UK.

ISBN 978-1-78398-286-8

www.packtpub.com

Credits

Authors
Emilien Kenler

Federico Razzoli

Reviewers
Aravinth C

Josh King

Pradeesh Parameswaran

Commissioning Editor
Kunal Parikh

Acquisition Editor
Vivek Anantharaman

Content Development Editor
Priyanka Mehta

Technical Editor
Siddhesh Ghadi

Copy Editors
Shruti Iyer

Sonia Mathur

Project Coordinator
Mary Alex

Proofreader
Safis Editing

Indexer
Mariammal Chettiyar

Graphics
Disha Haria

Production Coordinator
Arvindkumar Gupta

Cover Work
Arvindkumar Gupta

About the Authors

Emilien Kenler began focusing on game development after working on small web projects in 2008, when he was in High School. Until 2011, he worked for different groups and specialized in system administration.

A student of computer science engineering, Emilien founded a company that sold Minecraft servers in 2011. He created a lightweight IaaS (`https://github.com/HostYourCreeper/`) based on new technologies such as Node.js and RabbitMQ.

Thereafter, Emilien worked for TaDaweb as a system administrator, building its infrastructure and creating tools to manage deployment and monitoring.

In 2014, he began a new adventure at Wizcorp, Tokyo. In 2014, Emilien graduated from the University of Technology Compiègne, France.

He also contributed as a reviewer to *Learning Nagios 4*, *MariaDB High Performance*, *OpenVZ Essentials*, *Vagrant Virtual Development Environment Cookbook*, and *Getting Started with MariaDB Second Edition*, all by Packt Publishing.

Federico Razzoli is a software developer, database consultant, and free software supporter. He has been working on websites and database applications since 2000 and used MySQL and other relational databases extensively during this period. He is now a MariaDB Ambassador.

About the Reviewers

Aravinth C is a MySQL DBA at Mafiree with an experience of over 5 years.

Apart from MySQL, he is also good at shell scripting, Postgres, MongoDB, and Linux.

Pradeesh Parameswaran is a tech lover born and raised in Malaysia. He is passionate when it comes to technology and programming. Pradeesh has previously developed applications for Palm Handhelds and currently works for a telecommunication company in Malaysia. He is also pursuing his master's degree in Computer Science at the moment. In the future, Pradeesh plans to work towards making classrooms and learning much more interactive in order to help the underprivileged. He is a simple and humble guy who plans to change the world and make it a better place.

I would like to thank my parents for everything. You guys rock!

www.PacktPub.com

Support files, eBooks, discount offers, and more

For support files and downloads related to your book, please visit www.PacktPub.com.

Did you know that Packt offers eBook versions of every book published, with PDF and ePub files available? You can upgrade to the eBook version at www.PacktPub.com and as a print book customer, you are entitled to a discount on the eBook copy. Get in touch with us at service@packtpub.com for more details.

At www.PacktPub.com, you can also read a collection of free technical articles, sign up for a range of free newsletters and receive exclusive discounts and offers on Packt books and eBooks.

https://www2.packtpub.com/books/subscription/packtlib

Do you need instant solutions to your IT questions? PacktLib is Packt's online digital book library. Here, you can search, access, and read Packt's entire library of books.

Why subscribe?

- Fully searchable across every book published by Packt
- Copy and paste, print, and bookmark content
- On demand and accessible via a web browser

Free access for Packt account holders

If you have an account with Packt at www.PacktPub.com, you can use this to access PacktLib today and view 9 entirely free books. Simply use your login credentials for immediate access.

Table of Contents

Preface

Nowadays, computers are present everywhere, and they are all connected to each other. A lot of information is exchanged between them, but this data needs to be stored somewhere.

MariaDB is a fork of MySQL, started when MySQL was acquired by Sun Microsystems in 2008. Sun Microsytems and MySQL were then acquired by Oracle in 2009.

In most Linux distributions, MariaDB is now the default package, providing a relational database that is compatible with MySQL.

MariaDB has interesting new features, better testing, performance improvement, and bug fixes that are not available in MySQL.

This book provides an introduction to the SQL language. It presents some advanced features of MariaDB and features that aren't present in MySQL but come with MariaDB. By the end of this book, you should be able get your own MariaDB database server running and take advantage of its features.

What this book covers

Chapter 1, Installing MariaDB, describes the steps that need be taken before starting to use MariaDB.

Chapter 2, Databases and Tables, explains how to create data structures.

Chapter 3, Getting Started with SQL, covers the statements used to add, modify, or delete data in a database and the queries used to extract information.

Chapter 4, Importing and Exporting Data, explains how to import and export data.

Chapter 5, Views and Virtual Columns, presents views and virtual columns, which are used to shift the data logic from an application to a database.

Chapter 6, Dynamic Columns, explains how to store heterogeneous data in MariaDB using dynamic columns.

Chapter 7, Full-Text Searches, presents different ways to do full-text searches with MariaDB.

Chapter 8, Using the CONNECT Storage Engine, presents the CONNECT storage engine and ways to connect external data sources directly to MariaDB.

What you need for this book

To put the information provided in this book into practice, you need to install MariaDB on your computer. MariaDB runs on most operating systems, but the following are specifically mentioned in this book: Windows (from XP to Windows 8), Mac OS X, or a standard Linux distribution. Ubuntu, Debian, Mint, Fedora, CentOS, and Red Hat EL, among others, are also supported.

You will also need an Internet connection and the necessary administrative rights to install any software in order to install MariaDB.

No other software is required.

Who this book is for

If you don't know the SQL language but want to quickly jump into the SQL world and learn how to use MariaDB, this is the book for you.

Alternatively, if you already know how to use MySQL but want to go further into it in detail, this book is ideal for you. You will learn all the features added in MariaDB but absent in MySQL.

Conventions

In this book, you will find a number of text styles that distinguish between different kinds of information. Here are some examples of these styles and an explanation of their meaning.

Code words in text, database table names, folder names, filenames, file extensions, pathnames, dummy URLs, user input, and Twitter handles are shown as follows: "Create a `/tmp/mariadb/books2.xml` file following this structure."

A block of code is set as follows:

```
<book id="bk101">
    <author>
        <last>Gambardella</last>
        <first>Matthew</first>
    </author>
    <title>XML Developer's Guide</title>
    <genre>Computer</genre>
    <price>44.95</price>
    <publish_date>2000-10-01</publish_date>
    <description>An in-depth look at creating applications
    with XML.</description>
</book>
```

Any command-line input or output is written as follows:

```
SELECT WEEKDAY(date), COUNT(*)
  FROM product_order
  WHERE YEAR(date) = YEAR(NOW())
  GROUP BY WEEKDAY(date);
```

New terms and **important words** are shown in bold. Words that you see on the screen, for example, in menus or dialog boxes, appear in the text like this: "Clicking the **Next** button moves you to the next screen."

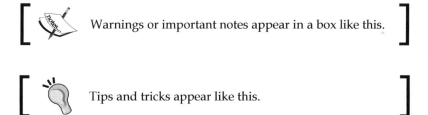

Warnings or important notes appear in a box like this.

Tips and tricks appear like this.

Reader feedback

Feedback from our readers is always welcome. Let us know what you think about this book—what you liked or disliked. Reader feedback is important for us as it helps us develop titles that you will really get the most out of.

To send us general feedback, simply e-mail feedback@packtpub.com, and mention the book's title in the subject of your message.

If there is a topic that you have expertise in and you are interested in either writing or contributing to a book, see our author guide at www.packtpub.com/authors.

Customer support

Now that you are the proud owner of a Packt book, we have a number of things to help you to get the most from your purchase.

Downloading the example code

You can download the example code files from your account at http://www. packtpub.com for all the Packt Publishing books you have purchased. If you purchased this book elsewhere, you can visit http://www.packtpub.com/support and register to have the files e-mailed directly to you.

Errata

Although we have taken every care to ensure the accuracy of our content, mistakes do happen. If you find a mistake in one of our books—maybe a mistake in the text or the code—we would be grateful if you could report this to us. By doing so, you can save other readers from frustration and help us improve subsequent versions of this book. If you find any errata, please report them by visiting http://www.packtpub.com/submit-errata, selecting your book, clicking on the **Errata Submission Form** link, and entering the details of your errata. Once your errata are verified, your submission will be accepted and the errata will be uploaded to our website or added to any list of existing errata under the Errata section of that title.

To view the previously submitted errata, go to https://www.packtpub.com/books/content/support and enter the name of the book in the search field. The required information will appear under the **Errata** section.

Piracy

Piracy of copyrighted material on the Internet is an ongoing problem across all media. At Packt, we take the protection of our copyright and licenses very seriously. If you come across any illegal copies of our works in any form on the Internet, please provide us with the location address or website name immediately so that we can pursue a remedy.

Please contact us at copyright@packtpub.com with a link to the suspected pirated material.

We appreciate your help in protecting our authors and our ability to bring you valuable content.

Questions

If you have a problem with any aspect of this book, you can contact us at questions@packtpub.com, and we will do our best to address the problem.

1
Installing MariaDB

MariaDB is a **Relational Database Management System (RDBMS)**. It is fully open source, released with a **GNU (General Public License)**, version 2. MariaDB is a fork of MySQL, started by its original author, *Michael Widenius* and some of MySQL's core developers.

Like other relational database management systems, MariaDB allows us to create and manage relational databases. It can modify the data structure and the data itself as well as answer questions (queries) on that data. The user can communicate with MariaDB by writing statements in **SQL (Structured Query Language)**. The statements can also be composed by a program, which can send them to MariaDB. This allows programs of any type, including web applications, to interact with MariaDB to manage their data.

This chapter describes the steps that need be taken before one starts using MariaDB. In particular, we will discuss the following topics:

- Choosing a MariaDB version
- Installing MariaDB on various operating systems
- Starting and stopping the server
- Configuring MariaDB
- Getting started with the command-line client
- Upgrading MariaDB
- Installing and configuring plugins

Choosing a MariaDB version

Choosing a MariaDB version is the first step to take. The MariaDB version numbers are composed of the following parts:

- A major version
- A minor version
- A patch number

The major and the minor versions identify a *tree*, for example: 10.0. Each new tree adds some features that were not in the previous tree, but could also add minor incompatibilities. Each patch fixes some bugs, and may introduce some minor features.

We generally want to install the latest stable tree. Older trees can be useful in the rare case where we need to run an application that is not compatible, or runs slower, with the most recent trees. Development trees are not stable, and should not be used in production. However, they are useful for testing new features before they become stable.

Before becoming stable, a tree goes through the following states:

- **Alpha**: In this state, the releases do not disturb the normal operations for most users, and contain the changes made in MySQL until at least the latest stable build
- **Beta**: At this stage, the tree contains all the features that were planned for this tree, and the API and storage formats are stable
- **Release candidate**: The tree is ready to be promoted as stable at this stage, but more testing is required.

At the time of writing, the most recent stable tree is 10.0, whereas a 10.1 development tree exists.

We always download the most recent release from the chosen tree. The older releases remain available for people who are affected by a recently introduced bug. However, before deciding to downgrade, consider that the recent versions may also fix security vulnerabilities.

The MariaDB documentation contains a list of the trees that are currently supported and a table showing when the support for current versions will be discontinued. The support also depends on the system on which MariaDB is installed, because very old versions of operating systems are not supported. This information is available at the following URL: `https://mariadb.com/kb/en/mariadb/development/deprecation-policy/`.

Installing MariaDB

Once we have chosen a MariaDB version, we can proceed to install it. This section covers the installation process on various systems.

All MariaDB packages can be downloaded from `https://downloads.mariadb.org/`. On Linux, a repository can be used to download the software and automate the upgrades. More details on this topic are provided in the *Installing on Linux* subsection.

Installing on Windows

MariaDB can be used on a Windows system in the following three ways:

- Normal installation
- Installation as a Windows service
- By using the `noinstall` package

Installing MariaDB as a service means that it will be started on system boot and stopped properly on system shutdown. If MariaDB is not installed as a service, we will need to start and stop it manually.

The noinstall package

The `noinstall` package is a ZIP archive that allows us to execute MariaDB on Windows systems without installing it. This is not the optimal way for executing MariaDB; however, this allows us to start using it quickly. For testing purposes, studying purposes, or for any trivial usage, a noinstall package can be acceptable.

To start using MariaDB without installation, all we have to do is to unpack the archive using a file archiver utility that is able to work with the ZIP format.

 A good open source program that we can use is 7-zip. It can be downloaded from `www.7-zip.org`.

MariaDB can be copied to any path, and any valid name can be used for its directory. Commonly used paths for MariaDB on Windows are `C:\MariaDB` and `C:\MariaDB 10.0`.

The package for Microsoft Installer

MariaDB can be installed on Windows from a `.MSI` package. It displays a graphical interface, which guides us through some simple steps, as follows:

1. Open the `.MSI` file to use the Windows installation wizard.

2. This allows us to install MariaDB normally or as a service. We will go through a series of simple steps. We are supposed to read the informative text and set some available options.

3. Click on the **Next** button. A **Back** button is also available in case we are not sure about the previously set options. A **Cancel** button allows us to abort the installation process.

The first step is merely a welcome text which informs us about the MariaDB version that we are going to install.

Then we are asked to accept the GPL license, which states the user's rights. We have a **Print** button here in case we prefer to read the license on paper.

To be able to go to the next step, we need to declare that we accept the license by checking the **I accept the terms in the License Agreement** checkbox, as seen in the following screenshot:

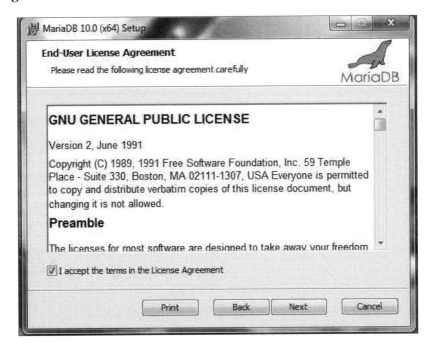

In the next step, we are asked to select the components to be installed. The component **Database instance** is necessary for a new installation. But this step can be skipped if we want to use an existing database, perhaps one created with an older version of MariaDB or with MySQL. However, in this case, please go through the *Upgrading MariaDB* section given later in this chapter for details.

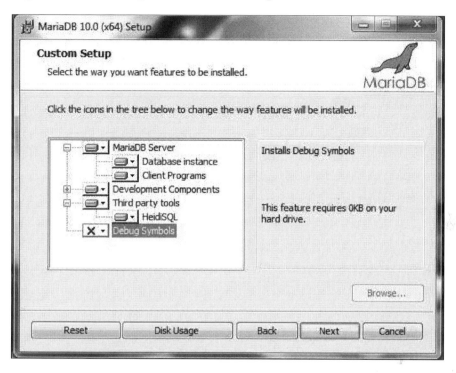

Then we are asked to set some basic options. First, we need to choose a password for the user root. We need to set this twice. If we skip this, the root user will have no password. This is acceptable if we are just installing MariaDB on our local machine for development purposes, but is usually a bad idea in other cases. Moreover, disabling remote access for the root user is usually recommended.

By creating an anonymous account, we allow non-authenticated users to access MariaDB. This can be convenient on a local development machine, but, again, this is generally a bad practice in other cases.

By default, MariaDB uses the `latin1` character set. This is usually acceptable for American users as well as many European users, though with `latin1`, it is not possible to store names using non-Latin character sets. Nowadays, in most cases, it is preferable to use `UTF8` or `UTF8MB4`.

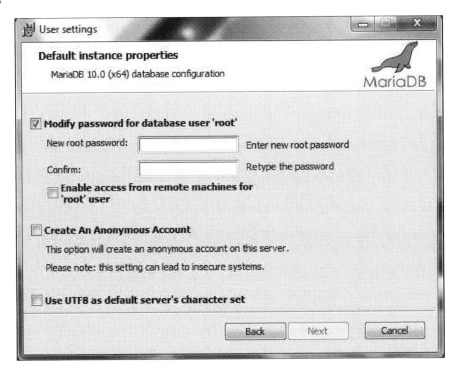

Now we need to decide if we want to install MariaDB as a service or not. If it is installed as a service, it starts at the time of system startup, and gracefully stops on system shutdown. In this case, the default name for the service is MySQL for compatibility reasons, but we can change it. We can also change the port number. The **Optimize for transactions** option should usually be checked. It means that InnoDB will be used as the default storage engine, which is the optimal choice in almost all situations. We are also asked to set the size for the InnoDB cache. For production purposes, it's a good choice to set it up at two-thirds of the available memory. It should also be able to contain all the data that we store in the InnoDB tables. If we are not sure, we can use the default value.

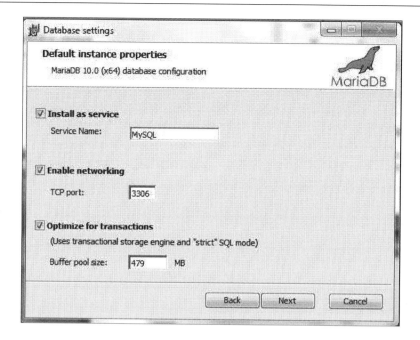

We are also asked if we want to install the **Feedback plugin**. This plugin, when active, periodically sends our database's usage statistics to the MariaDB project servers. No private data is sent.

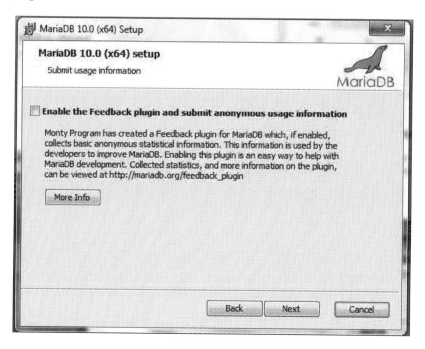

Finally, MariaDB is installed, and we receive a message that informs us that the installation was successful.

Installing on Linux

Some Linux distributions include MariaDB in their repositories. If we use one of those distributions, we can easily install MariaDB with a trivial command-line statement or even a graphical utility. In this case, we can check our system's documentation to find out the way to install MariaDB or, more generally speaking, any software package.

However, we may prefer to use the official MariaDB packages and the official MariaDB repositories. If we do so, we can choose any of the MariaDB versions. Moreover, the official repositories guarantee that we are constantly up-to-date with the latest features and bug fixes.

The MariaDB-generic Linux binaries are also available. These packages can be used on any Linux distribution for which a specific package is not available. They also allow a more customized installation: for example, with these binaries, we can install MariaDB in any path we choose. However, note that, if we choose to use a generic binary, we will need to take care of the dependencies.

Using official repositories

If we want to use the MariaDB official repositories, we need to configure our system before installing MariaDB.

The MariaDB Foundation provides a web wizard that allows us to do this by following very easy steps. This tool is available at the following URL:

```
https://downloads.mariadb.org/mariadb/repositories/
```

First, we must inform the tool about what we are using and what we want to install. The following screenshot shows the tool:

We will just need to follow four simple steps:

- **Choose a Distro**: Click on the name of the Linux distribution. For example: **Mint**.

- **Choose a Release**: Click on the name of the version of our Linux distribution. For example: **Min 17 "Qiana"**.

- **Choose a Version**: Choose the MariaDB version that we want to install. For example: **10.0**.

- **Choose a Mirror**: This is optional, because a mirror is already selected. However, we can choose a mirror that is closer to us, or another mirror if we find it slow.

At this point, in the lower part of the page, we can see the exact steps to be followed for setting up the specified official mirror in our system. The steps to install MariaDB may or may not be included. If they are not, we will follow one of the next sections, or our system's documentation.

The .deb packages

The .deb packages are used in Debian GNU/Linux and in all the derived Linux distributions, including Ubuntu. These packages can be installed using apt-get, aptitude, or the graphical package manager synaptic. These tools are generally preinstalled in the distributions derived from Debian.

We can install the mariadb-server and mariadb-client meta-packages to install the most recent stable MariaDB version that is available in the repository, including the command-line clients and tools. The following packages are optional but useful, and provide features that will be discussed in this book:

- mariadb-connect-engine-10.0: The CONNECT storage engine
- mariadb-oqgraph-engine-10.0: The OQGRAPH storage engine

We can update the local list of packages, and then install MariaDB using apt-get using the following commands:

```
sudo apt-get update
sudo apt-get upgrade
sudo apt-get install mariadb-server mariadb-client mariadb-connect-engine-10.0 mariadb-oqgraph-engine-10.0
```

Note that this code snippet includes the optional packages mentioned previously.

The .rpm packages

The .rpm packages are used in Linux distributions derived from Red Hat, including the community distribution Fedora, the enterprise-level CentOS, SuSE, and Mandriva. To manage these packages, we can use the YUM or up2date tools.

To install the latest version of the MariaDB server and client tools, we need to install the MariaDB-server and MariaDB-client, as follows:

```
sudo yum update
sudo yum install MariaDB-server MariaDB-client
```

Installing MariaDB on Gentoo

Installing MariaDB on Gentoo Linux is very simple. We can use the emerge package to install the proper eBuild. The code is as follows:

```
emerge –sync
emerge --ask mariadb
```

Only in cases where we want MariaDB to automatically start on system boot, can we run the following:

```
rc-update add mysql default
```

Generic Linux binaries

The MariaDB generic binaries can be useful for installing MariaDB on Linux distributions and other UNIX systems for which a specific package does not exist. Moreover, advanced users can modify the general installation procedure to customize the installation.

Users who install MariaDB from generic binaries for Linux/UNIX should be aware of two aspects:

* They will need to take care of the dependencies manually
* MariaDB updates will not be automatic

The following procedure should work on all Linux systems. If a problem occurs, we should check our system's documentation.

```
useradd -r mysql
cd /usr/local
tar zxvf /path/to/<package_name>
ln -s <mariadb_dir> mysql
cd mysql
chown -R mysql .
chgrp -R mysql .
scripts/mysql_install_db --user=mysql
chown -R root .
chown -R mysql data
```

We will need to replace <package_name> with the name of the file, and <mariadb_dir> with the name of the file without the .tar.gz extension.

Note that, with this procedure, we can install any number of MariaDB or MySQL versions. Each version will have its own subdirectory inside /usr/local. A symbolic link called /usr/local/mysql will point to the version of MariaDB/MySQL in use. Also note that, with this procedure, each installation will have its own data directory, which means that data will not be shared. The data directory should be configured in the my.cnf file. You also need to configure a different port or Unix socket for each instance if you want to run them at the same time.

Installing on MacOS

The best way to install MariaDB on a MacOS X system is by using Homebrew. It is an unofficial, yet high-quality, open source package manager for MacOS. It is written in the Ruby language, and it requires Apple Xcode, which can be installed from the Apple Store.

So, if Homebrew is not installed on our system, first we need to install it. The following line usually does the trick:

```
ruby -e "$(curl -fsSL https://raw.githubusercontent.com/Homebrew/install/
master/install)"
```

To make sure that the setup was successful, we may execute this command:

```
brew doctor
```

If we have problems, we can refer to the Homebrew online documentation at the following URL:

```
https://github.com/Homebrew/homebrew/wiki
```

With Homebrew properly installed, we need to update the packages list and install MariaDB. We can do this with commands that are similar to those supported by Debian's `apt-get`:

```
brew update
brew install mariadb
```

Starting and stopping MariaDB

Depending on how MariaDB is installed, it may or may not start automatically at system startup. On Linux, it starts automatically if it is installed using the deb or rpm package. On Windows, it starts automatically if it is installed as a service. Whether or not MariaDB starts automatically, we will be able to start and stop it manually using the command line. The executable files that we need to call, as well as the client and other tools, are situated in the MariaDB binary directory. Since typing this path every time is not convenient, we will add it to the system paths.

On Linux, this is done by adding the path to the `$PATH` variable, as in the following example:

```
export PATH=$PATH:/usr/local/bin
```

However, this change will be lost when the current user logs out. To make it permanent, we must add the preceding line to the `.profile` start in our home directory, like in the following example:

```
echo 'export PATH=$PATH:/usr/local/mysql/bin' >> .bash_profile
```

On Windows, the procedure to add a path to the PATH variable is easy but it depends on the system version. Here we will see how to add the MariaDB path on Windows 8:

1. Open the **Control Panel**. Click on the **System** icon, and then on **Advanced**. Click on the **Environment Variables** button. Select PATH, and modify it in the **Edit** window. Add the path to your MariaDB binary directory. Click on **OK**.

On other Windows versions, we can check the system's documentation for the correct procedure to use.

Now we can start MariaDB by invoking the server executable, as follows:

```
mysqld
```

This command starts a MariaDB demon, the programs which will remain active and waiting for client connections. However, this is not the recommended way to start MariaDB on Linux/UNIX systems. Instead, we can run the `mysqld_safe` script, which starts `mysqld`, and constantly checks if it is active. If `mysqld` crashes, `mysqld_safe` tries to restart it. It can be invoked in the following way:

```
mysqld_safe
```

Many options can be passed to `mysqld` or `mysqld_safe`. Most of them should only be used by advanced users and only on rare occasions; thus, they are beyond the purpose of this book. However, we will see some basic options in the *Configuring MariaDB* section of this chapter. Meanwhile, we can simply start MariaDB with the default values.

To stop MariaDB, we need a user with the SHUTDOWN privilege. We will pass the user's credentials (username and password) to the `mysqladmin` utility along with the shutdown option. So, provided that the password for the root user is saoirse, the following example will work:

```
mysqladmin shutdown -uroot -psaoirse
```

The `-u` option specifies a username, and the `-p` option specifies a password. Note that no space is needed after these options.

Sometimes, it could be more convenient to use the SHUTDOWN SQL command, as shown in the following example:

```
MariaDB [(none)]> SHUTDOWN;
Query OK, 0 rows affected (0.00 sec)
MariaDB [(none)]> SELECT version();
ERROR 2006 (HY000): MySQL server has gone away
No connection. Trying to reconnect...
ERROR 2002 (HY000): Can't connect to local MySQL server through socket
'/tmp/mysql.sock' (2 "No such file or directory")
ERROR: Can't connect to the server
```

Getting started with the mysql client

Now that we've installed MariaDB, and we know how to start it, we are ready to open the client and start running our first SQL statements!

In this book, we will use the mysql command-line client to run SQL statements. Many open source graphical clients are available for free. They provide an easy way to perform most operations without the need for remembering the syntax of all the SQL statements. The actions performed on the graphic interface are internally converted to SQL statements. Most of these clients also provide the ability to manually type the statements for execution. However, by manually typing the SQL statements into mysql we will always exactly know what we are doing. Additionally, once we accumulate some experience, this method will probably be the faster one in most situations.

In this section, we will learn to start and quit the command-line client, run statements, and to use the client commands.

Starting and quitting the client

To start the client, we need to specify at least the username and the password that we want to use for this session. The options to do this are the same as we used earlier for mysqladmin. The following example shows how to start mysql and the typical output that appears on the screen:

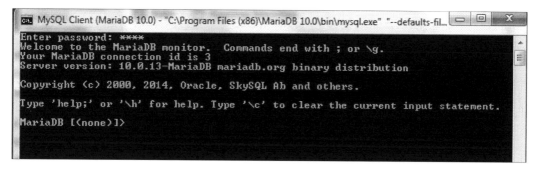

Now the client is running in an interactive mode, which means that we can enter queries and it will show us an output. When we want to quit the client, we can type the \quit command or its brief version, \q.

```
MariaDB [test]> \quit
Bye
```

There are two non-interactive ways to use the command-line client as well. One of them is to pass it a single statement. The client will send the query to the server, which will show us the output and then terminate. This is useful if we do not have other statements to execute. The -e option can be used to pass a query to mysql, like in the following example:

```
federico@this:~$ /usr/local/mysql/bin/mysql -uroot -psaoirse -e "SELECT
VERSION()"
+---------------------+
| VERSION()           |
+---------------------+
| 10.0.13-MariaDB-log |
+---------------------+
```

It is also possible to pass the path of a text file containing the SQL statements to MySQL for execution. The client will read the file, execute all the commands, and show us the output. We can do this with a system-independent syntax:

```
mysql -uroot -proot < 1.sql
```

Running queries

Let's look at the prompt, the final line in the preceding example. It starts with the words: MariaDB. This is useful, because the mysql client also allows us to connect to the MySQL databases. But this string informs us that we are connected to MariaDB. Then we see none, which means that no default database is selected.

This means that, in our SQL statements, we always have to specify a database name. For example, if we want to list all the tables in a database, we will type the following:

```
MariaDB [(none)]> SHOW TABLES FROM test;
+-----------------+
| Tables_in_test  |
+-----------------+
| _xy             |
+-----------------+
1 rows in set (0.00 sec)
```

With a view to typing less verbose statements, when working with a database we can select it with the USE command. Consider the following example:

```
MariaDB [(none)]> USE test;
Database changed
MariaDB [test]> SHOW TABLES;
+-----------------+
| Tables_in_test  |
+-----------------+
| _xy             |
+-----------------+
1 rows in set (0.00 sec)
```

As we can see from these examples, to run an SQL statement, we just need to type it into the mysql command line. We can separate the words with any number of spaces, tabs, and new line characters. The client knows that a statement is finished when it finds a delimiter, which is, by default, the semicolon character (;). It is even possible to write more than one statement in one line. Take a look at the following two examples:

```
MariaDB [test]> SELECT
    -> VERSION();
+---------------------+
| VERSION()           |
```

```
+--------------------+
| 10.0.13-MariaDB-log |
+--------------------+
1 row in set (0.00 sec)
MariaDB [test]> SELECT VERSION(); SELECT PI();
+--------------------+
| VERSION()          |
+--------------------+
| 10.0.13-MariaDB-log |
+--------------------+
1 row in set (0.00 sec)
+----------+
| PI()     |
+----------+
| 3.141593 |
+----------+
1 row in set (0.00 sec)
```

In all the preceding examples, the output of the queries is shown in tabular form. But when an output contains many columns, it can be useful to print it vertically. This can be done by terminating a statement with the character, \G instead of a semicolon. For example:

```
MariaDB [test]> SHOW CHARACTER SET LIKE 'ascii' \G
*************************** 1. row ***************************
          Charset: ascii
      Description: US ASCII
Default collation: ascii_general_ci
           Maxlen: 1
1 row in set (0.00 sec)
```

Even if the client is running in interactive mode, we can still execute the SQL statements from a test file by using the SOURCE command:

```
SOURCE my_file.sql;
```

In the Linux and UNIX systems, `mysql` maintains a history of the statements that we execute. We can recall such statements and execute them again. To move backwards and forward through the statement history, we can use the *arrow up* and *arrow down* keys. You can also use *Ctrl + R*, as in any standard shell, to do a reverse search in the history.

Client commands

In the previous examples, we used some client commands, such as `\q` (or `\quit`) to leave the client, and `\G` to get the output displayed vertically. A client command is a statement that affects the behavior of `mysql` in some way. These commands are never sent to the server. Most client commands are brief strings starting with the backslash character (`\`), though USE and SOURCE are client commands too. Here we will see the most useful commands.

The `\h` command, or `\help`, shows a list of the available client commands.

Sometimes, we want to completely delete the statement we are typing because of an error. A faster way to achieve the same result is by using the `\c` command and pressing *Enter*. `mysql` will simply ignore the line, and will not send it to the server.

The `\W` command (upper case) causes server warnings to be shown in the command line along with fatal errors. The `\w` causes warnings to be hidden, but errors will still appear. While the default behavior hides the warnings, examining them could be important to find out if a problem occurs during the execution of statements.

On Linux, `\P` can be used to set a pager. A **pager** is a program used to see statement results. For example, if a query produces large results, we can use less as a pager to be able to scroll through the results. Then, `\n` can be used to unset the pager. For example:

```
MariaDB [(none)]> \P less
PAGER set to 'less'
MariaDB [(none)]> SELECT * FROM information_schema.COLUMNS \G
2042 rows in set (0.68 sec)
MariaDB [(none)]> \n
PAGER set to stdout
```

On the Linux and UNIX systems, we can use the `\e` command to compose a statement in an external editor such as Vim or GNU Emacs. The choice of the editor depends on the `$EDITOR` system variable.

With the system or \! command, we can execute a system command, and see its output on the screen. This can be useful in several situations. For example, if we want to install a plugin but we do not remember the file name, we can use one of the following commands to list the contents of the `plugin` directory:

```
system ls /usr/local/mysql/lib/plugin/
\! ls /usr/local/mysql/lib/plugin/
```

Configuring MariaDB

The MariaDB behavior is affected by a number of server variables. Before discussing the important variables, it is necessary to understand how to set such variables.

The values of the server variables are set in the following ways:

* For each variable, there exists a default value.

* One or more configuration files can be read by MariaDB at startup. Each file sets some variables, overriding the default values.

* `mysqld` can be called with some options. In this case, each option overrides the value of a server variable.

* At runtime, it is still possible to change the values of some variables. These variables are called **dynamic variables**. The values of **static variables** cannot be changed at runtime; thus, modifying such variables requires a server restart.

* Some variables exist in the global and session context. This means that every session can have a specific value for those variables. In this case, the global value serves as the default: when a new session is created, its value is copied from the global value. The session value can be changed later. Changing the global value does not affect existing connections but only new ones.

Configuration files

As explained earlier, MariaDB can read more than one configuration system. On startup, MariaDB accesses some paths in a predetermined order, seeking configuration files. Each file overrides the settings that were previously read from other files.

The paths in which MariaDB looks for configuration files are system-dependent. On Linux, it reads the following paths, in the given order:

- `/etc`
- `/etc/mysql`
- `SYSCONFDIR`
- `$MYSQL_HOME`
- The file indicated with the `--defaults-extra-file` option
- `~/`

On Windows, the following paths are read:

- `%PROGRAMDATA%\MariaDB\MariaDB Server 10.0`
- `%WINDIR%`
- `C:\`
- MariaDB installation directory
- The file indicated with the `--defaults-extra-file` option

On Linux, configuration files are expected to be called `my.cnf`. On Windows, they can be called `my.ini` or `my.cnf`.

Note that installers create a default configuration file with values that are usually acceptable if we want to develop applications with MariaDB on our local machine only. On Linux, this file is usually located in `/etc`.

For each file, MariaDB reads the following option groups in the same order (replace `x.x` with the proper version number, for example 10.0):

- `[mysqld]`
- `[server]`
- `[mysqld-X.X]`
- `[mariadb]`
- `[mariadb-X.X]`
- `[client-server]`

The client-server group is very useful, because it is read by both the client and the server. This allows specifying the parameters that need to be used by both (for example, the port number or the path for the socket file) only once.

The following minimal example shows the syntax to be used in the configuration files:

```
[client-server]
port=3306
socket=/tmp/mysql.sock
```

Passing options to mysqld

As mentioned before, it is possible to pass options to mysqld at startup. These options override the settings in the configuration files. On Linux, the same options can also be passed to mysqld_safe, which will pass them to mysqld.

The names of the command-line options are very similar to the configuration files options, except that they generally begin with a double dash (-), and use dashes as word separators instead of underscores (_).

For example, the innodb_buffer_pool_size server variable determines the size of the main MariaDB cache in bytes. It can be set in the configuration files with this syntax:

```
innodb_buffer_pool_size = 134217728
```

This setting can be overridden with a startup option using the following syntax:

```
mysqld --innodb-buffer-pool-size=134217728
```

Or by using mysqld_safe:

```
mysqld_safe --innodb-buffer-pool-size=134217728
```

Setting server variables at runtime

A server variable is a setting whose value somehow affects the behavior of MariaDB. If a variable is only global, its value applies to all the connections or to some internal mechanism of the server. If a corresponding session variable exists, each session value affects a particular connection. The global value is still important, because it represents the initial value for the session variable. However, modifying a global variable affects only new connections; the corresponding session variables will remain untouched for the existing connections.

Also note that we can only modify dynamic variables. We can read the value of static variables, but trying to modify them will cause an error.

Server variables can be read and modified using the SELECT and SET SQL statements.

If we need to read or modify a session variable, we can use the following syntax:

```
MariaDB [(none)]> SET @@session.sql_mode = 'strict_trans_tables';
Query OK, 0 rows affected (0.00 sec)
MariaDB [(none)]> SELECT @@session.sql_mode;
+---------------------+
| @@session.sql_mode  |
+---------------------+
| STRICT_TRANS_TABLES |
+---------------------+
1 row in set (0.00 sec)
```

Similarly, to read or modify a global variable, we will use the following syntax:

```
MariaDB [(none)]> SET @@global.sql_mode = 'no_zero_date';
Query OK, 0 rows affected (0.00 sec)
MariaDB [(none)]> SELECT @@global.sql_mode;
+-------------------+
| @@global.sql_mode |
+-------------------+
| NO_ZERO_DATE      |
+-------------------+
1 row in set (0.00 sec)
```

Some global variables, but not all, can be set to their default value by specifying DEFAULT instead of a value. It is possible to set a session variable to the value of the corresponding global variable with the same syntax.

Upgrading MariaDB

If a package manager has been used to install MariaDB, the patch upgrades, like 10.0.12 to 10.0.13, are automatic. Each package manager supports a command to upgrade the packages, and will also take care to upgrade the dependencies if needed. If no package manager is used (for example, when we are working on Windows or if we have installed the generic Linux/UNIX binaries), we will need to manually uninstall and re-install MariaDB. This is also true for minor or major version upgrades such as 10.0 to 10.1. The following commands can be used with the package managers that have been used in this chapter:

- With `apt-get` (Debian):

  ```
  sudo apt-get update
  sudo apt-get upgrade
  ```

- With `Yum` (Red Hat):

  ```
  sudo yum update MariaDB-server MariaDB-client
  ```

- With `emerge` (Gentoo):

  ```
  emerge -avDuN mariadb
  ```

- With Homebrew (MacOS X):

  ```
  brew upgrade mariadb
  ```

Usually, we want the new version to read our old database. So, first we need to set up the data directory, which is the directory in which the databases are written by default. A common path is `/var/mysql`. To use this path, we will add the following line in the configuration file:

```
datadir=/var/mysql
```

This setting will not take effect until MariaDB is restarted.

At this point, we need to upgrade the format of our databases. Since the data has been written with an older release, some modifications to the files could be necessary before the new version of MariaDB can read it. For this purpose, MariaDB distributions include a tool called `mysql_upgrade`. This must be done even if a package manager has been used for upgrading MariaDB.

The `mysql_upgrade` tool must be run when the server is running. It reads the options from the configuration files. However, if the login credentials are not written in the configuration files, the typical invocation for `mysql_upgrade` is the following:

```
mysql_upgrade -u<user_name> -p<password>
```

Replace `<user_name>` with a valid username and `<password>` with the corresponding password.

After running `mysql_upgrade`, we will be able to work again without databases!

Managing plugins

MariaDB has several functionalities, but more can be added by installing plugins. This allows the users to deactivate some unneeded functionality by uninstalling a plugin, or activating functionalities that are not needed by the majority of users. More importantly, some plugins implement the same class of functionalities in different ways. This is the case with **storage engines**, a special plugin type that will be discussed in *Chapter 2, Databases and Tables*. Some plugins are developed by the MariaDB team, others by individuals or companies that are members of the community. Several plugins, developed by the MariaDB team or by third parties, are included in the official MariaDB distributions. Others are available at their respective developer's websites.

Plugins are contained in files with the `.so` extension on Linux and with the `.ddl` extension on Windows. Each file is a library that can contain one or more plugins. These files need to be located in the plugins directory. To discover the path of such a directory in our MariaDB installation, we can query the `@@plugin_dir` server variable:

```
MariaDB [(none)]> SELECT @@plugin_dir;
+------------------------------+
| @@plugin_dir                 |
+------------------------------+
| /usr/local/mysql/lib/plugin/ |
+------------------------------+
1 row in set (0.00 sec)
```

MariaDB provides some SQL statements to manage plugins at runtime. The following list shows these statements, before discussing them in detail:

- `SHOW PLUGINS` displays a list of available plugins
- `INSTALL SONAME` installs all the plugins from a file
- `UNINSTALL SONAME` uninstalls all the plugins contained in a library
- `INSTALL PLUGIN` installs an individual plugin
- `UNINSTALL PLUGIN` uninstalls an individual plugin

The syntax of SHOW PLUGINS is very simple. Consider the following example:

```
MariaDB [(none)]> SHOW PLUGINS;
+-------------------------------+----------+---------------------+-----------
-----------+---------+
| Name                          | Status   | Type                | Library
| License |
+-------------------------------+----------+---------------------+-----------
-----------+---------+
| binlog                        | ACTIVE   | STORAGE ENGINE      | NULL
| GPL     |
| mysql_native_password         | ACTIVE   | AUTHENTICATION      | NULL
| GPL     |
| mysql_old_password            | ACTIVE   | AUTHENTICATION      | NULL
| GPL     |
...
+-------------------------------+----------+---------------------+-----------
-----------+---------+
54 rows in set (0.00 sec)
```

The list has been truncated because it was very long. However, from the example, we can see that five columns are returned by this statement:

- Name: Plugin name.
- Status: ACTIVE means that the plugin is installed, INACTIVE means that the plugin is not installed, DISABLED means that the plugin has been disabled with a server option and cannot be installed, and DELETED means that the library file has been removed.
- Type: This value indicates the plugin type. For example, the value AUTHENTICATION means that the plugin handles the user's login, and INFORMATION SCHEMA means that the plugin provides metainformation to the user.
- Library: This indicates the library file name. If this value is NULL, the plugin is built-in and cannot be uninstalled.
- License: Indicates the plugin's license, which determines the user's rights. This is just the license name: the complete text should be provided as a file distributed along with the plugin.

If a library contains more than one plugin, we will want to install them all to enable the whole set of related functionalities. For this reason, we will usually prefer the INSTALL SONAME statement. The name of the file must be passed to this statement. The file extension is optional, which allows us to install a library on any system using the identical command. For example, to install the SEQUENCE storage engine, we use the following command:

```
INSTALL SONAME 'ha_sequence';
```

Similarly, we can uninstall the whole set of plugins with UNINSTALL SONAME, like in the following example:

```
UNINSTALL SONAME 'ha_sequence';
```

In very rare cases, we may want to install or uninstall a single plugin. In such cases, we will use the INSTALL PLUGIN or UNINSTALL PLUGIN statement, specifying the name of the plugin that we want to install or uninstall, and the file name. For example:

```
INSTALL PLUGIN sequence SONAME 'ha_sequence';
UNINSTALL PLUGIN sequence;
```

Some plugins create a set of server variables that can be used to configure them at runtime. Such variables do not exist until the plugin is installed or after it is uninstalled. By convention, usually all these variables have the same prefix, which is the plugin name. This makes it easier to discover them with the SHOW VARIABLES statement. The following example shows how this mechanism works:

```
MariaDB [(none)]> SHOW VARIABLES LIKE 'spider%';
Empty set (0.00 sec)

MariaDB [(none)]> INSTALL SONAME 'ha_spider';
Query OK, 0 rows affected (0.01 sec)

MariaDB [(none)]> SHOW VARIABLES LIKE 'spider%';
+------------------------------------------+-------+
| Variable_name                            | Value |
+------------------------------------------+-------+
| spider_auto_increment_mode               | -1    |
| spider_bgs_first_read                     | -1    |
...
+------------------------------------------+-------+
99 rows in set (0.00 sec)
```

Summary

In this chapter, we discussed the preliminary tasks that we need to perform before we can start working with MariaDB. In particular, we discussed the way to choose a MariaDB version and install it. We learned how to start and stop MariaDB, and how to efficiently use the `mysql` command-line client. Several other clients exist, but this is the one we will use for all the examples in this book. We learned how to set the MariaDB options in the configuration files or at the mysqld invocation. Some settings can be set at runtime, and sometimes they can be adjusted on a per-session basis: we discussed how to do this. MariaDB upgrades were also been discussed in the chapter. Finally, we learned how to install, uninstall, and configure MariaDB plugins.

In the next chapter, we will learn how to create new databases and tables, the data types that are available, how storage engines work, and the use of indexes.

2
Databases and Tables

In the previous chapter, we learned how to install and update MariaDB, and we started playing with `mysql`, its command-line client. In this chapter, we will learn how to create the data structures on which we want to work. We will use the MariaDB server that we installed in the previous chapter, and use the already explained command-line client. We will also create an example database that will be used in the rest of the book.

In particular, we will cover the following topics:

* Working with databases
* Working with tables
* Data types
* Character sets and collations
* Storage engines
* Indexing
* Using comments
* Working with metadata
* Creating an install script

Working with databases

An RDBMS allows you to store data in a structured way, with relations between the different data collections. These collections of data are stored in tables. However, each table is located in a database. We can see this structure as a container for tables and other objects. In MariaDB, **schema** is a synonym for database and is used in the documentation as well as in the statement syntax.

To list the existing databases, we can use the SHOW DATABASES statement. Let's try it on our newly installed MariaDB:

```
MariaDB [(none)]> SHOW DATABASES;
+--------------------+
| Database           |
+--------------------+
| information_schema |
| mysql              |
| test               |
+--------------------+
3 rows in set (0.09 sec)
```

As we can see in this code snippet, there are several built-in databases. They are as follows:

- information_schema: A virtual database containing various meta-information about our data structures and server usage. It can be read, but not directly modified.

- mysql: This is the system database that is internally used by MariaDB. Modifying it is highly discouraged, and can cause damage.

- test: This is an empty database that we can use for our tests.

> From MariaDB 5.5 onwards, the performance_schema database is also available. It provides performance-monitoring features by collecting server events.

We can now add a database with the CREATE DATABASE command:

```
MariaDB [(none)]> CREATE DATABASE eshop;
Query OK, 1 row affected (0.01 sec)
MariaDB [(none)]> SHOW DATABASES;
+--------------------+
| Database           |
+--------------------+
| eshop              |
| information_schema |
| mysql              |
| test               |
+--------------------+
4 rows in set (0.00 sec)
```

We can also erase the `test` database to keep our data cleaner. For this, we can use
`DROP DATABASE`:

```
MariaDB [(none)]> DROP DATABASE test;
Query OK, 0 rows affected (0.00 sec)
MariaDB [(none)]> SHOW DATABASES;
+--------------------+
| Database           |
+--------------------+
| eshop              |
| information_schema |
| mysql              |
+--------------------+
3 rows in set (0.00 sec)
```

 Be careful with this statement, because it completely destroys a database and all the tables that it contains.

`SHOW SCHEMAS`, `CREATE SCHEMA`, and `DROP SCHEMA` can also be used as substitutes for
these statements.

Working with tables

Now we are going to create the necessary tables. First, we will run the `USE` statement
to set eshop as our default database. This allows us to avoid specifying the database
name in each statement, as explained in *Chapter 1, Installing MariaDB*.

```
MariaDB [(none)]> USE eshop;
Database changed
```

Then we can create our first table using `CREATE TABLE`. This command specifies
concepts that have not yet been discussed, such as table types and storage engines. The
following example shows the syntax of the statement, but we will leave out the details
for now. All these concepts will be made clear by the end of this chapter.

```
CREATE TABLE catalogue
(
  id INTEGER UNSIGNED NOT NULL AUTO_INCREMENT,
  name VARCHAR(50) NOT NULL,
  price DECIMAL(6, 2) NULL,
```

```
  quantity SMALLINT NOT NULL DEFAULT 0,
  description TEXT NOT NULL,
  PRIMARY KEY (id)
)
  ENGINE = InnoDB
  COMMENT 'Catalogue of products on sale';
```

While the details are probably a bit obscure, the general syntax of the statement is simple. After the TABLE keyword, we have the table name. Between the parentheses, the individual column definitions come first, separated by commas. Then there are usually some index definitions; in this example only the primary key is defined. After the parenthesis, we see the table options but they are not mandatory. The whole statement is also called a **table definition**.

The SHOW TABLES statement can be used to get a list of all the tables in the default database:

```
MariaDB [eshop]> SHOW TABLES;
+-----------------+
| Tables_in_eshop |
+-----------------+
| catalogue       |
+-----------------+
1 row in set (0.00 sec)
```

We called the table catalogue in the previous code snippet. Although a catalogue generally contains products, this name is a bit too vague. We can change it using the RENAME TABLE statement:

```
MariaDB [eshop]> RENAME TABLE catalogue TO product;
Query OK, 0 rows affected (0.25 sec)
```

We can also create a table with a structure identical to the structure of another table. The new table will be empty.

```
MariaDB [eshop]> CREATE TABLE product_2 LIKE product;
Query OK, 0 rows affected (0.40 sec)
```

Finally, tables can be erased with the DROP TABLE command, as follows:

```
MariaDB [eshop]> DROP TABLE product_2;
Query OK, 0 rows affected (0.22 sec)
```

Be careful with this statement: it completely destroys a table and its contents.

We can also create temporary tables. This is useful for data that belongs to a specific user and need not to be stored permanently. Temporary tables can only be accessed by their creator. When the user disconnects or MariaDB is stopped, all temporary tables are lost.

To create temporary tables, we can use the keyword, TEMPORARY:

```
CREATE TEMPORARY TABLE ...
```

A temporary table can have the same name as a non-temporary table. In this case, the temporary table will hide the regular table for the current session, or until it is dropped.

The DROP TABLE and ALTER TABLE statements work with both temporary and regular tables. However, to be sure to run them on temporary tables and prevent mistakes, we can add the TEMPORARY keyword, as follows:

```
ALTER TEMPORARY TABLE ...
DROP TEMPORARY TABLE ...
```

Working with columns

A table row can be seen as a collection of named properties are called **columns** or **fields**. So, columns must suit the units of data that make up the information.

In the previous sections, we learned the most important SQL statements for managing databases and tables. We have also seen some example column definitions. In this section, we will discuss the following:

- Column definitions
- The management of columns

A column definition has the following syntax:

```
<column_name> <data_type> [type_attributes] [NULL | NOT NULL]
[DEFAULT <value>] [AUTO_INCREMENT] [COMMENT 'string']
```

The following subsections will explain the data types, the NULL attribute, and the default values. The AUTO_INCREMENT attribute and comments will be discussed later in the indexing section of this chapter.

Data types

The data type is the most important characteristic that we need to set: it determines the class of data that the column will contain, its size, the way it will be stored, and the operations that will be allowed on it.

MariaDB supports the following macro-classes of data types:

- String types
- Numeric types
- Date and time types
- ENUM and SET types
- Geometric data

The Geometric data types are representations of geometric shapes following the OpenGIS standard. They are mostly used for geographic searches. This class of type will not be discussed in this book.

String types

String types are meant to store characters or sequences of characters. A string value in MariaDB is quoted using single quotes (`'string'`). Single quote characters between the quotes need to be *escaped* with a backslash (\'). For this reason, backslashes are special characters too; if we want to include them in strings, we need to escape them with another backslash (\\).

```
MariaDB [(none)]> SELECT 'Hello World!' AS one, 'This is a \' char' AS
two, '\\' AS three;
+--------------+-------------------+-------+
| one          | two               | three |
+--------------+-------------------+-------+
| Hello World! | This is a ' char  | \     |
+--------------+-------------------+-------+
1 row in set (0.00 sec)
```

Note that the type is expressed in bytes and not in characters. As we will discuss later in the section on *Character sets and collations*, the number of bytes necessary to store a character depends on the character set. Moreover, rows have a maximum length in MariaDB. This limit depends on the storage engine used. With the default engine (InnoDB), this limit is 65,535 bytes. This limit does not apply to the TEXT and BLOB columns, which are stored separately. But the size limit of VARCHAR is purely theoretical, because it is equal to the maximum row size.

A string type can be dynamic or have a fixed length. If the type is dynamic, each data will only occupy the necessary space. If it is fixed, each data will occupy the same length. The Dynamic types often save space, but they can result in slower queries.

Values of the binary types are compared and ordered as sequences of bytes and not as characters. Binary types can be used, for example, to store images, videos, or audio records.

The following table lists the string types:

Data type	Max size	Dynamic	Binary	Notes
CHAR	255 characters	No	No	The size must be specified by the user
VARCHAR	65,535 bytes	Yes	No	The size must be specified by the user
BINARY	255 bytes	No	Yes	The size must be specified by the user
VARBINARY	65,535 bytes	Yes	Yes	The size must be specified by the user
TINYTEXT	2^8 bytes	Yes	No	Does not affect the row size
TEXT	2^{16} bytes	Yes	No	Does not affect the row size
MEDIUMTEXT	2^{24} bytes	Yes	No	Does not affect the row size
LONGTEXT	2^{32} bytes	Yes	No	Does not affect the row size
TINYBLOB	2^8 bytes	Yes	Yes	Does not affect the row size
BLOB	2^{16} bytes	Yes	Yes	Does not affect the row size
MEDIUMBLOB	2^{24} bytes	Yes	Yes	Does not affect the row size
LONGBLOB	2^{32} bytes	Yes	Yes	Does not affect the row size

The size for the CHAR, VARCHAR, BINARY, and VARBINARY columns can be specified as a number. For example:

```
CHAR(20)
```

Numeric types

MariaDB has several data types that can be used to store numbers. Each of them accepts two modifiers: SIGNED and UNSIGNED. If a column is defined as UNSIGNED, it can only contain positive numbers or zero. However, the maximum value that can be stored in an INTEGER UNSIGNED is double the maximum value of an INTEGER SIGNED. By default, all the numbers are stored as signed numbers as described by the SQL standard.

The SIGNED and UNSIGNED modifiers are MariaDB - and MySQL specific. In standard SQL, numbers can always be negative.

Numeric values should always be written without quotes so that MariaDB understands that they are not strings. However, in most cases, MariaDB understands when values need be converted to numbers. Look at the following example:

```
MariaDB [(none)]> SELECT 1 AS one, 1 + '1' AS two;
+-----+-----+
| one | two |
+-----+-----+
|   1 |   2 |
+-----+-----+
1 row in set (0.00 sec)
```

The following integer types are supported:

Data Type	Size
TINYINT	1 byte
SMALLINT	2 bytes
MEDIUMINT	3 bytes
INTEGER (or INT)	4 bytes
BIGINT	8 bytes

 Note that INTEGER and INT are synonyms.

Non-integer types can be stored efficiently using the floating point types. These values are written with a dot (.) to separate the integer part from the decimal part. Any of the two parts (but not both) can be omitted if they are zero. For example:

```
MariaDB [(none)]> SELECT 0.0 AS one, .1 AS two, 1. AS three;
+-----+-----+-------+
| one | two | three |
+-----+-----+-------+
| 0.0 | 0.1 |     1 |
+-----+-----+-------+
1 row in set (0.00 sec)
```

It is important to remember that manipulating these values, even with the simplest arithmetical operation, returns an approximate result. This means that the rightmost digits of a float value are not reliable.

There are two floating point types:

- `FLOAT`, which takes four bytes
- `DOUBLE` (or `DOUBLE PRECISION`), which takes eight bytes

Another way to store decimal numbers is the `DECIMAL` (or `NUMERIC`) type. Numbers stored in this way are internally represented as strings, so these values are always exact. A `DECIMAL` column can be declared with the following syntax:

```
DECIMAL(digits, decimal_part)
```

In the preceding command, `digits` is the total number of digits to store, including both the integer and the decimal part of the numbers, and `decimal_part` is the number of decimal digits to be stored. So, the following example can store numbers within the range `0.00` to `9.99`, with no more than two decimal digits:

```
DECIMAL(3, 2)
```

Each part of the number requires the number of bytes that is equal to its size divided by two (and rounded up to the closest integer if necessary).

> Numbers that refer to money, such as product prices, should always be declared as `DECIMAL`. The `FLOAT` and `DOUBLE` types should not be used for this purpose because of their lack of precision; this is a common pitfall for beginners.

Temporal types

MariaDB supports the following temporal types:

Data type	Size in bytes	Notes
TIMESTAMP	4	Seconds elapsed since 1970/01/01. Only the TIMESTAMP columns can have the current time as the default value
DATETIME	8	
DATE	3	
TIME	3	
YEAR	1	

A TIMESTAMP data type represents the seconds elapsed since 1970/01/01 (UNIX epoch). This value is also known as the **UNIX timestamp**. Only the TIMESTAMP columns can have the current time as the default value. It is written as an integer, without quotes.

The TIME data type is rarely used. A common pitfall is to consider it as a daytime value. Instead, it indicates a number of hours, minutes, and seconds in the range from '-838:59:59' to '838:59:59'.

YEAR is a non-standard and a very uncommon type. However, it allows us to store the year values in one byte, saving some storage space and making searches faster. It should be written as a four-digit integer.

Other types can be written as strings. By default, dates are written in the YYYY-MM-DD format, and time is written in the HH:HH:SS format. To avoid ambiguities, the following standard SQL format is also allowed for dates, times, and timestamps, respectively:

- DATE 'YYYY-MM-DD'
- TIME 'HH:MM:DD'
- TIMESTAMP 'timestamp'

MariaDB parses the temporal strings in a very flexible way; thus, it is possible to use different separators, omit separators, and specify years in a two-digit format as long as there is no ambiguity.

A microsecond precision is allowed for the TIMESTAMP, DATETIME, and TIME formats. To define a column that can store the fractional parts of a second, the following syntax can be used:

TIMESTAMP (precision)

In the preceding command, precision indicates the number of decimal digits that are allowed. The minimum is 0 (no decimal digits), and the maximum is 6 (microseconds). Fractions of seconds are written like floating point numbers:

```
MariaDB [mwa]> SELECT NOW(6);
+----------------------------+
| NOW(6)                     |
+----------------------------+
| 2014-09-16 18:57:25.056860 |
+----------------------------+
1 row in set (0.00 sec)
```

ENUM and SET types

MariaDB supports the non-standard ENUM and SET types. Both of these can assume values from a list specified by the user. The difference is that an ENUM column always has one, and only one, value from the list. A SET column has any number of values at the same time, including zero. The values in the list must be strings. It is also possible to use their index, starting from 1, without the quotes. The values are always extracted as strings.

For example, consider the following example in which we define a color column:

```
MariaDB [mwa]> CREATE TABLE enum_example
    -> (
    -> color ENUM('white', 'black', 'green', 'blue') DEFAULT 'white'
    -> );
Query OK, 0 rows affected (0.41 sec)
MariaDB [mwa]> INSERT INTO enum_example (color) VALUES (1);
Query OK, 1 row affected (0.08 sec)
MariaDB [mwa]> INSERT INTO enum_example (color) VALUES ('black');
Query OK, 1 row affected (0.08 sec)
MariaDB [mwa]> SELECT color FROM enum_example;
+-------+
| color |
+-------+
| white |
| black |
+-------+
2 rows in set (0.00 sec)
```

NULL values

Independently from the data types, columns can be declared as NULL or NOT NULL. The default option is NULL, which means that the column can contain NULL values.

NULL is a special value or, more strictly speaking, a pseudo-value. Academic people had long discussions about its meaning: some think that NULL always indicates an unknown value, while others think that it can represent the absence of a value. In any case, it should not be confused with the so-called empty value, such as zero or an empty string.

Most operators and functions return NULL if one of the operands or parameters is NULL. In fact, we cannot know the result of an operation, if we don't know one of the values involved. This general rule is not always applicable, because some operators and functions are specifically designed to work with NULL. The most important operators of this type will be discussed in *Chapter 3, Getting Started with SQL*.

Columns should be declared as NOT NULL when possible. There are at least two reasons for this:

- NULL could be the result of a wrong expression. By forbidding NULL values for a column, we can avoid junk rows, and obtain an error when an unexpected NULL appears.
- Searches on the NOT NULL columns are slightly faster.

The following is an example of a column that cannot contain NULL values:

```
last_name CHAR(50) NOT NULL
```

Default values

Columns can optionally have a default value. This means that, when a new row is inserted in the table and no value is explicitly assigned to the column, the default value will be written. Default values are constant values, not expressions. The only exception are the TIMESTAMP columns, which can have the current timestamp as a default value.

If a column does not have a default value, and no value is explicitly assigned, the behavior of MariaDB will depend on the @@sql_mode server variable. This aspect will be explained in detail in *Chapter 3, Getting Started with SQL*.

The following is an example of a column with a default value:

```
price INTEGER UNSIGNED DEFAULT 0
```

For the TIMESTAMP columns, the following optional clauses can be specified in any order:

- DEFAULT CURRENT_TIMESTAMP indicates that the new rows have the current timestamp as default values. Any other constant valid value can also be specified.
- ON UPDATE CURRENT_TIMESTAMP indicates that when a row is modified, by default the column's value is updated to the current timestamp. This clause cannot specify a value other than CURRENT_TIMESTAMP. If this clause is present, DEFAULT must be specified too.

However, note that, for both the clauses, setting the current timestamp is the default behavior.

Character sets and collations

MariaDB supports several character sets, or charsets, and collations.

A charset is a class of characters and a way to translate them into bytes. Each character set includes letters and strings of one or more alphabets and, usually, some symbols. Character sets have a length, which depends on the number of characters that they include. Some character sets have a variable length, which means that some characters require more bytes than the others. Smaller character sets are more efficient. Variable-length character sets are generally less efficient; however, the variable length is an important feature that notably reduces the size of strings, because most common characters are smaller.

Each character set has a number of collations. A collation determines the order of the characters, and whether two characters are equal. Generally, at least a case-sensitive and a case-insensitive collation exists. For example, a case-sensitive collation considers 'A' and 'a' as equal. A case-sensitive collation determines which one comes first when ordering a string alphabetically. Since the same characters can be sorted in several ways (in different countries, or even in the same country), there are multiple collations for each character set. Complex collations are slower than simple collations.

Each text column uses a character set and a collation. Different columns can use different character sets and collations, even within the same table. If a character set is not explicitly specified for a column, the table's default character set is used. If that has not been specified, the database's default character set is used. If this too was not specified, the server's default character set is used, which is determined by the `@@character_set_server` variable. By default, it is `utf8`.

An identical mechanism applies to collation. The server's default collation is determined by `@@collation_server`. If a character set was specified, at any level, but the collation was not, the character set's default collation is used.

The following is an example of a column definition that includes a character set and collation:

```
name CHAR(50) CHARACTER SET 'utf8' COLLATE 'utf8_unicode_ci'
```

To specify the default character set and collation for a table, execute the following:

```
CREATE TABLE example
(
...
)
  CHARACTER SET 'utf8'
  COLLATE 'utf8_unicode_ci';
```

To specify the default character set and collation for a database, give the following command:

CREATE DATABASE test2 CHARACTER SET 'utf8' COLLATE 'utf8_unicode_ci';

Keep in mind that comparing different collations or character sets is not always possible. When it is possible, MariaDB has to convert one of them internally. This operation takes time. For this reason, in general it is not a good idea to use different character sets within the same database.

To see which character sets and collations are available, we can use these statements:

```
SHOW CHARACTER SET;
SHOW COLLATION;
```

To see the collations whose name starts with a given prefix, we can use the LIKE clause. For example:

```
SHOW COLLATION LIKE 'utf8%';
```

This is useful because the names of collations start with the name of the character sets that they refer to. Moreover, their names end with cs or ci to indicate if they are case-sensitive or case-insensitive, respectively.

So, which character set should we choose? It depends. In most cases, the best choice is utf8, which is a universal character set; it even includes some dead alphabets and several symbols. In most cases, its default collation (utf8_general_ci) is a good choice. It is fast but, in some rare cases, it is less correct than utf8_unicode_ci. With modern processors, we can choose to ignore the performance difference. But remember that these collations are not compatible. To reduce the size of our data, we can choose a smaller character set. The Maxlen column in the output of SHOW CHARACTER SETS indicates the maximum size of a single character.

Storage engines

MariaDB does not directly write or read table data. Such operations are delegated to a special type of plugin called **storage engines**. This is the same mechanism that is used in MySQL. In fact, storage engines written for MySQL can be recompiled against MariaDB, and vice versa.

Storage engines can also support features that are not directly supported by the server. For example:

- Transactions
- Data and index caches
- Foreign keys

When we create a table, we should decide which storage engine will be used for handling the table. We can then specify it with the ENGINE table option, as we did in the *Working with Tables* section:

```
CREATE TABLE table_name
(
    ...
)
    ENGINE = InnoDB;
```

The preceding clause is optional. If it is not specified, the @@storage_engine server variable will determine the storage engine to be used. This variable can also be set per session. By default, it is set to InnoDB:

```
MariaDB [(none)]> SELECT @@storage_engine;
+------------------+
| @@storage_engine |
+------------------+
| InnoDB           |
+------------------+
1 row in set (0.01 sec)
```

 Starting from MariaDB 10.1, which is currently not stable, the storage engine used for temporary tables is determined by the @@default_tmp_storage_engine variable.

Just like all plugins, storage engines can be installed and uninstalled dynamically. Storage engines are displayed by the SHOW PLUGINS statement. However, the following specific command only shows storage engines:

```
SHOW ENGINES;
```

The following storage engines are the most commonly used ones:

Storage engines	Description
InnoDB	It is the fastest and the most reliable storage engine for the majority of use cases. Unlike other storage engines, it also supports row-level locking and transactions, and is ACID-compliant, which guarantees reliability. When we are not sure which storage engine we should use, InnoDB is generally the best choice. In fact, MariaDB includes XtraDB, which is a fork of InnoDB with performance improvements.
MyISAM	This storage engine has been heavily battle-tested, since it was introduced and used as the default storage engine in MySQL several years ago. It can be faster than InnoDB with big tables in a read-intensive workload. MyISAM is not crash-safe, but it is faster than Aria for write operations.
Aria	Aria is a new storage engine, developed as a crash-safe replacement for MyISAM. It is also suitable for big tables that are not frequently modified. Currently, it does not support transactions, but if MariaDB crashes during a statement execution, the last version of data (just before the statement) can always be recovered. In the future, Aria's developers want to make it ACID-compliant and support transactions.
MEMORY	This storage engine keeps the tables in memory, and does not write anything to disk. If MariaDB is stopped or crashes, all data in the MEMORY tables is lost. However, this storage engine is very fast. Generally, it is a good choice for temporary data that needs to be accessed intensively.
BLACKHOLE	A BLACKHOLE table is the relational equivalent of the Linux/dev/null file. Data inserted into these tables is lost, and nothing can be read from them. As the name suggests, this storage engine acts like a black hole!

Other storage engines will be discussed in the following chapters of this book.

Indexing

Operations on databases can be complex. Often, MariaDB has to examine several data to find the rows that we want to read. It may also have to perform complex operations, such as aggregating data or sorting values. Typical operations on data will be described in *Chapter 3, Getting Started with SQL*. Here we will briefly discuss the data structure used to optimize these operations—that is, **indexes**. **Key** is a synonym for index.

> Note that different storage engines implement indexes in different ways. The following discussion refers to InnoDB, which is the most commonly used engine. If we use other engines, such as MEMORY or MyISAM, we may need to check the MariaDB KnowledgeBase to learn how these engines handle indexes.

To explain what an index is, we are going to use a typical example: a book's index. Imagine we have to find a topic, or some specific information, in a big book that we have never read before, and which does not have an index. We would need a lot of time! But fortunately, books have indexes. So, imagine searching for a topic using the analytical index. It is easy: topics are listed alphabetically, and when we find the desired topic, we can see the page number of the topic that we want to read. Pages have progressive numbers, so finding it will be easy.

Table indexes are very similar to book indexes. They are ordered structures which contain the data to be searched along with the unique identifiers of the structures containing the specific data that we are looking for. Incidentally, those data structures are called **pages**.

Let's see how this happens from the user's point of view. Usually, tables contain a **primary key**: a unique and not null index which contains a column, or a set of columns, whose values uniquely identify individual rows. The primary key is frequently built on a single column which contains progressive numbers, automatically generated by MariaDB using the AUTO_INCREMENT clause. By convention, this column is called id.

Other indexes can be built on any other column or set of columns. They contain the values of these columns, plus the corresponding values of the primary key.

So, suppose we have a table containing information about our company's employees. We have an id column (the primary key), an indexed column called last_name, and several other columns. Suppose that we ask MariaDB to extract the row corresponding to a specific last name, 'Jones'. MariaDB will search 'Jones' in the index built on the last_name column. The desired entry contains the value of the id column corresponding to the desired table row. Since rows are physically sorted by id, finding and extracting the row corresponding to the employee called Jones will be a fast operation.

The following code creates a table with the desired indexes:

```
CREATE TABLE employee
(
  id SMALLINT UNSIGNED AUTO_INCREMENT PRIMARY KEY,
  first_name CHAR(50),
  last_name CHAR(50),
  INDEX idx_last_name (last_name)
)
  ENGINE = InnoDB;
```

There are some details that should be highlighted in this example:

- Primary keys cannot contain NULL values. That is why we did not declare id as NOT NULL: this attribute is implicit. However, if we want to explicitly declare it as NOT NULL, we can do it.

- id is declared as AUTO_INCREMENT. This means that it contains progressive numbers automatically generated by MariaDB. AUTO_INCREMENT generates the numbers in a series that starts from 1 by default, and can never be lower than 0. You can only have one AUTO_INCREMENT column by table.

- id is of type SMALLINT. Some beginners always use the BIGINT type for primary keys to make sure that the maximum value is never reached. However, this can be a waste of space and slow down the queries. It is preferable to use smaller types unless BIGINT is really needed.

- Indexes have names. If we do not explicitly assign a name to an index, MariaDB will automatically generate one.

As noted earlier, primary keys cannot contain NULL values. They also have another important restriction: they cannot contain duplicate values. Trying to insert a NULL or a duplicate value will cause an error.

MariaDB supports other indexes that reject duplicate values: unique indexes. Declaring such indexes is useful when we do not want a column, or a set of columns, to contain duplicate values. For example, if we have a table containing information about a website's users, we would usually want to be sure that each user is registered with a different e-mail address. Sometimes, unique indexes are defined to enforce data integrity, even if they are not especially useful in making queries faster.

Unique indexes can be declared using the UNIQUE keyword:

```
UNIQUE INDEX [index_name] (<columns>)
```

> Many beginners tend to create many indexes, because they do not know which of them will really be useful. The developers of some of the most common web applications make this mistake as well. The reason why this is a bad idea is that using many indexes is a waste of storage space, and slows down the write operations.

Using comments

When creating a complex database, we often need to write some notes that remind us what the various objects are, and why we made certain design choices. Of course we can write this note on a file or even on paper if we prefer. But the best place to keep notes is with the database itself. For this purpose, we can use comments.

Comments are strings that are associated with a certain data structure. They can be set for columns, indexes, tables, or other objects that we have not yet discussed. In all cases, we will use a COMMENT clause to specify comments:

```
CREATE TABLE example
(
  column1 CHAR(1) NOT NULL DEFAULT ''
    COMMENT 'This is a column comment',
  INDEX idx1 (column1) COMMENT 'An index comment'
)
  COMMENT 'This table is just an example';
```

Working with metadata

Sometimes, we may want to check the structure of an existing table. For a user, the quickest way is often the SHOW CREATE TABLE statement. This command returns the CREATE TABLE statement that can be used to recreate an identical table. For example:

```
MariaDB [test]> SHOW CREATE TABLE example \G
*************************** 1. row ***************************
       Table: example
Create Table: CREATE TABLE `example` (
  `column1` char(1) NOT NULL DEFAULT '' COMMENT 'This is a column
comment',
  KEY `idx1` (`column1`) COMMENT 'An index comment'
) ENGINE=InnoDB DEFAULT CHARSET=utf8 COMMENT='This table is just an
example'
1 row in set (0.00 sec)
```

However, parsing a CREATE TABLE statement is a hard task for programs. For this reason, the following two commands return a table's metadata as a relational table:

- SHOW COLUMNS FROM <table_name> (or DESC <table_name>) provides information about the columns
- SHOW KEYS FROM <table_name> provides information about the indexes

Creating an installation script

When we develop an application that interacts with a database, we need to create a script that recreates the same database structure on other computers. The creation of the application database is part of the installation process.

This database install script is usually a text file that contains the SQL commands to create the database. By convention, this file has a .sql extension. As mentioned in *Chapter 1*, *Installing MariaDB*, the most common way to execute a file containing queries is by passing it to the mysql command-line client. For example:

```
mysql -uroot -pmypassword < install_db.sql
```

The fastest way to create such a script is by using `mysqldump`. This tool, mainly used to create backups, will be discussed in detail in *Chapter 4, Importing and Exporting Data*. It produces SQL files called **dumps**. The basic syntax to create a dump from a single database is as follows:

```
mysqldump [options] db_name > <file_name>
```

If we only want to have the statements that create the data structures, without the table contents, we can use the `--no-data` option.

For example, let's take a look at the way to obtain the SQL statements that recreate the structure of the `eshop` database. These statements will be written in the `eshop.sql` file:

```
mysqldump -uroot -pmypassword --no-data eshop > eshop.sql
```

After doing this, the file can be manually edited with any text editor if necessary.

If we have a very low number of tables, we may prefer to obtain these statements using the following commands:

- `SHOW CREATE DATABASE <db_name>;`
- `SHOW CREATE TABLE <table_name>;`

Till now, the process is quite simple. But what if several versions of our application exist with each version having introduced differences in the database? We do not want to create a different script for each version: it would be an overcomplicated task for us, and it would add complexity to the install process. Thus, we need to create a script that does the following:

- Create the database if it does not exist;
- Update the database structure if it is old
- Nothing if the database structure is already up-to-date

Normally, trying to create an object that already exists results in an error. The same happens when trying to destroy an object that does not exist. When an error occurs, the execution of the SQL file stops. This means that, if we use the CREATE, DROP, and ALTER statements as they were used in the previous examples, we need to know the exact current structure of the database. But we probably don't.

In this case, MariaDB helps us with some interesting clauses that can be used with some CREATE, DROP, and ALTER statements. Let's take a look at them.

Clause	Can be used with	Description
IF NOT EXISTS	CREATE DATABASE CREATE TABLE ALTER TABLE ... ADD COLUMN ALTER TABLE ... CHANGE COLUMN ALTER TABLE ... MODIFY COLUMN ALTER TABLE ... ADD INDEX	If the specified object does not yet exist, it is created. Otherwise, nothing happens.
IF EXISTS	DROP DATABASE DROP TABLE ALTER TABLE ... DROP COLUMN ALTER TABLE ... DROP INDEX	If the object exists, it is destroyed. Otherwise, nothing happens.
OR REPLACE	CREATE TABLE	If the table does not exist, it is created. If it exists, it is destroyed and recreated.

These clauses are supported by several other statements that we have not yet discussed. When such statements are explained, these special clauses will be mentioned.

Let's see some examples:

```
-- add column2 if it does not exist
ALTER TABLE example ADD COLUMN IF NOT EXISTS column2 CHAR(2);
-- if the column already exists, change its definition
ALTER TABLE example MODIFY COLUMN IF EXISTS column2 CHAR(2);
-- drop index idx1 if it exists
ALTER TABLE example DROP INDEX IF EXISTS idx1;
```

These clauses are not a part of any standard SQL specification.

However, IF EXISTS and IF NOT EXISTS have been supported by MySQL since the 90s, and some other SQL implementations, such as PostgreSQL and SQLite, support them as well. However, only MariaDB implements them in this way for ALTER TABLE. PostgreSQL provides a generic ALTER TABLE IF EXISTS, which avoids returning an error if a table does not exist.

The OR REPLACE clause is an Oracle proprietary extension, later implemented in PostgreSQL as well. MariaDB plans to support it more extensively in its future releases.

Summary

In this chapter, we discussed the main topics that concern database and table creation. We learned to manage databases, the objects which contain all the other data structures.

Then we learned to manage tables and the columns and indexes that they contain. While doing this, we discussed the various data types supported by MariaDB, as well as character sets and collations.

Finally, we learned how to create an SQL file for installing or upgrading a database.

Until now, we've only discussed data structures. We have not exhausted the topic yet, but we covered the main structures. In the next chapter, we will start working with data itself.

3
Getting Started with SQL

In the previous chapters, we learned how to install MariaDB, and to create a database with some tables. Now that we know how to do this, we can use MariaDB for its main purpose: working with data!

In this chapter, we will discuss the statements used to add, modify, or delete data in the database as well as the queries to extract the information that we need. We will cover the following topics in this chapter:

- Working with rows
- Understanding transactions
- Foreign keys
- Dealing with duplicate rows and other errors
- Reading rows
- Joining tables
- Working with operators
- Working with time and date values
- Comments

Working with rows

In this section, we will discuss how to write data in MariaDB. Any general-purpose storage system implements four basic operations that are summarized with the acronym **CRUD**:

- **Create**: the addition of a new item
- **Read**: obtaining information about an item
- **Update**: Modifying information about an existing item
- **Delete**: Deletion of an existing item

The **Read** operation is the most complex and will be discussed in the *Reading rows* section, later. But first, we need to write some data into our database. So this section focuses on the `Create`, `Update`, and `Delete` operations. Enforcing data integrity is also a fundamental functionality of a relational DBMS, so we will also discuss it here.

Inserting rows

In *Chapter 2*, *Databases and Tables*, in the *Working with tables* section, we created a table called `product` that contains information about the products on sale in our online shop. Of course, when a table is created, it is empty. It has columns and indexes meant to store data, but it does not have any rows as yet. So, let's insert our first row.

The statement used to insert new rows into a table is, not surprisingly, `INSERT`. MariaDB supports two different syntaxes for this command. Let's try the easier one first with an example:

```
INSERT INTO product
SET name = 'T-Shirt', price = 20.00, quantity = DEFAULT, description =
'';
```

With the `DEFAULT` keyword, we explicitly indicate that `quantity` must be set to its default value. The same goal can be achieved by simply omitting the column. In fact, we omitted the `id` column; since that column has the `AUTO_INCREMENT` attribute, MariaDB will fill it with a progressive number value.

The syntax included in the standard SQL specifications is slightly different. The following example inserts exactly the same data:

```
INSERT INTO product (name, price, quantity, description)
VALUES ('T-Shirt', 20.00, DEFAULT, '');
```

This syntax can be a little harder to read or write, because the field names are listed separately from the list of values. This can make the correspondence harder to find when inserting several values. However, only the standard syntax allows you to insert more than one row with one command. This can be done in the following way:

```
INSERT INTO product (name, price, quantity, description) VALUES
('Black T-Shirt', 25.00, DEFAULT, ''),
('Red T-Shirt', 25.00, DEFAULT, '');
```

In this way, we can insert a huge number of rows with a single statement. This greatly reduces client/server communication, resulting in a much higher speed.

Now, let's check the rows we inserted using the former commands:

```
MariaDB [test]> SELECT * FROM product;
+----+---------------+-------+----------+-------------+
| id | name          | price | quantity | description |
+----+---------------+-------+----------+-------------+
|  1 | T-Shirt       | 20.00 |        0 |             |
|  2 | T-Shirt       | 20.00 |        0 |             |
|  3 | Black T-Shirt | 25.00 |        0 |             |
|  4 | Red T-Shirt   | 25.00 |        0 |             |
+----+---------------+-------+----------+-------------+
4 rows in set (0.00 sec)
```

The SELECT statement will be discussed in detail later, in the *Reading rows* section. We have used it in its simplest form: we simply asked for all the data present in the product table.

Modifying rows

It is possible to modify existing rows with the UPDATE statement. Let's see an example before discussing the syntax:

```
UPDATE product SET price = 15.00 WHERE id = 2;
```

SQL is very similar to English, so this example is almost self-explanatory. Let's analyze it. The statement consists of the following pieces of information:

- A table name: In this case, we are going to modify zero or more rows from the product table.

- The WHERE clause specifies the rows we are going to modify. In this case, MariaDB will search for rows whose id is 2. Any valid SQL expression is allowed here so, for example, we could modify the rows having a price lower than 50 and a quantity higher than 0. But we will learn the syntax to do this later in this chapter, in the *Operators and functions* section. This clause is optional: if it is omitted, all the rows will be modified.

- The SET clause specifies the changes that MariaDB should apply to each of the matching rows. We already know this clause, because we used it with the INSERT statement. For an UPDATE statement, SET is mandatory.

So, to summarize, the preceding command asks MariaDB to set a price of 15 for the product whose id is 2.

Let's check if it worked as expected:

```
MariaDB [test]> SELECT * FROM product;
+----+---------------+-------+----------+-------------+
| id | name          | price | quantity | description |
+----+---------------+-------+----------+-------------+
|  1 | T-Shirt       | 20.00 |        0 |             |
|  2 | T-Shirt       | 20.00 |        0 |             |
|  3 | Black T-Shirt | 15.00 |        0 |             |
|  4 | Red T-Shirt   | 20.00 |        0 |             |
+----+---------------+-------+----------+-------------+
4 rows in set (0.00 sec)
```

Yes, it did!

Deleting rows

We learned to insert new rows and to modify the existing ones. Now, the only missing fundamental operation is the deletion of an existing row. To delete rows, we will use the DELETE statement. Again, let's learn it with an example:

```
DELETE FROM product WHERE id = 1;
```

This statement is even simpler than the UPDATE statement. First, we specify the table that contains the rows to be deleted. Then we provide a WHERE clause, similar to the one that we used with the UPDATE statement. Again, the WHERE clause is optional: if it is omitted, all the rows are deleted, and the table is emptied completely.

So, this statement asks MariaDB to delete the rows in the product table whose id is 1.

An interesting clause that we can use is RETURNING. It can be used to obtain information about the deleted rows. Usually, this option is used by programs, and not by users directly. For example, applications can use it to log the IDs of the deleted rows in a separate table. Or, perhaps, a program could display the information about the rows being deleted. More generally, the applications can use RETURNING as a shortcut; that is, instead of performing a SELECT query followed by DELETE, they can just perform a DELETE with RETURNING. When executing a large number of statements, reducing them can be an important optimization.

Again, let's see an example:

```
MariaDB [test]> DELETE FROM product WHERE price <= 20 RETURNING id,
price;
+----+-------+
| id | price |
+----+-------+
|  1 | 20.00 |
|  2 | 15.00 |
+----+-------+
2 rows in set (0.08 sec)
```

We asked MariaDB to delete the rows where the price is less than or equal to (<=) 20. We also asked MariaDB to show us the id and price values of each deleted row.

Understanding transactions

A **transaction** is a sequence of SQL statements that are grouped into a single logical operation. Its purpose is to guarantee the integrity of data. If a transaction fails, no change will be applied to the databases. If a transaction succeeds, all statements will succeed.

Why is this so important? Consider the following example:

```
START TRANSACTION;
SELECT quantity FROM product WHERE id = 42;
UPDATE product
  SET quantity = quantity - 10
  WHERE id = 42;
UPDATE customer
  SET money = money -
  (SELECT price FROM product WHERE id = 42)
  WHERE id = 512;
INSERT INTO product_order
  (product_id, quantity, customer_id)
  VALUES (42, 10, 512);
COMMIT;
```

We haven't yet discussed some of the statements used in the preceding example. However, they are not transactions we need to understand. This sequence of statements happens when a customer (whose `id` is `512`) orders a product (with `id 42`). As a consequence, we need to execute the following sub-operations in our database:

- Check that the desired quantity of products is available. If it is not, we should not proceed.
- Decrease the available quantity of items for the product that is being bought.
- Decrease the amount of money in the online account of the customer.
- Register the order, so that the product will be delivered to the customer.

These sub-operations form a more complex operation. When a session is executing this operation, we do not want other connections to interfere. Imagine a scenario like this:

1. Connection A checks how many products with id 42 are available. Only one is available, but it is enough.
2. Immediately after that, connection B checks the availability of the same product. It finds that one is available.
3. Connection A decreases the quantity of the product. Now it is 0.
4. Connection B decreases the same number. Now it is -1.
5. Both connections create an order. Two customers will pay for the same product. But only one is available!

This is something we definitely want to avoid. But there is another situation that we want to avoid. Imagine that the server crashes immediately after a customer's money is deducted. The order will not be written into the database, and the customer will end up paying for something that he will not receive.

Fortunately, transactions prevent both these situations. They protect our database writes in two ways:

- During a transaction, relevant data is locked or copied. In both cases, two connections will not be able to modify the same rows at the same time.
- The writes will not be made effective until the COMMIT command is issued. This means that, if the server crashes during the transaction, all the sub-operations will be rolled back. We will not have inconsistent data (such as payment for a product that will not be delivered).

In this example, the transaction starts when we issue a START TRANSACTION command. Then, any number of operations can be performed. The COMMIT command makes the changes effective.

This does not mean that, if a statement fails with an error, the transaction is always aborted. In many cases, the application will receive an error, and will be free to decide whether the transaction should be aborted or not. To abort the current transaction, an application can execute the ROLLBACK command.

Note that a transaction can consist of only one statement. This makes perfect sense, because the server could crash in the middle of the statement's execution.

The autocommit mode

In many cases, we don't want to group multiple statements within a transaction. When a transaction consists of only one statement, sending the START TRANSACTION and COMMIT statements can be annoying. For this reason, MariaDB has an autocommit mode.

The autocommit mode is ON by default. Unless a START TRANSACTION command is explicitly used, the autocommit mode causes an implicit commit after each statement. Thus, every statement is executed in a separate transaction by default.

When the autocommit mode is OFF, a new transaction implicitly starts after each commit, and the COMMIT command needs be issued explicitly.

To turn the autocommit ON or OFF, we can use the @@autocommit server variable:

```
MariaDB [mwa]> SET @@autocommit = OFF;
Query OK, 0 rows affected (0.00 sec)
MariaDB [mwa]> SELECT @@autocommit;
+--------------+
| @@autocommit |
+--------------+
|            0 |
+--------------+
1 row in set (0.00 sec)
```

The limitations of a transaction in MariaDB

Transaction handling is not implemented in the core of MariaDB; instead, it is left to the storage engines. Many storage engines, such as MyISAM or MEMORY, do not implement it at all. The following are the transactional storage engines:

- InnoDB;
- XtraDB;
- TokuDB

 In a sense, tables in Aria are partially transactional. While Aria ignores commands such as START TRANSACTION, COMMIT, and ROLLBACK, each statement is something of a transaction. In fact, if it writes, modifies, or deletes multiple rows, the operation completely succeeds or completely fails like a transaction.

Only statements that modify data can be used inside a transaction. Statements that modify a table structure (such as ALTER TABLE) implicitly commit the current transaction.

Sometimes, we may not be sure if a transaction is active or not. Usually this happens when we are not sure if autocommit is set to ON or not, or if the latest statement implicitly committed a transaction. In these cases, the @in_transaction variable can help us. Its value is 1 if a transaction is active and 0 if it is not. Here is an example:

```
MariaDB [mwa]> START TRANSACTION;
Query OK, 0 rows affected (0.00 sec)
MariaDB [mwa]> SELECT @@in_transaction;
+------------------+
| @@in_transaction |
+------------------+
|                1 |
+------------------+
1 row in set (0.00 sec)
MariaDB [mwa]> DROP TABLE IF EXISTS t;
Query OK, 0 rows affected, 1 warning (0.00 sec)
MariaDB [mwa]> SELECT @@in_transaction;
```

```
+------------------+
| @@in_transaction |
+------------------+
|                0 |
+------------------+
1 row in set (0.00 sec)
```

 InnoDB is optimized to execute a huge number of short transactions. If our databases are busy and performance is important for us, we should try to avoid big transactions in terms of the number of statements and execution time. This is particularly true if we have several concurrent connections reading the same tables.

Foreign keys

As you know, relationships exist between the tables in a relational database. This means that the rows in a table are usually associated to the rows in another table or multiple tables.

Creating relationships between tables

Let's see an example. Suppose that our online store sells several types of products. We don't want to display them all together, because it would be confusing for most users. Instead, we need to separate our products by category.

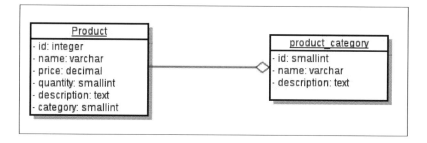

So, first we will create a table for the product categories. We need to store the category name, a description, and of course an id that will be the primary key:

```
CREATE TABLE product_category
(
  id SMALLINT UNSIGNED AUTO_INCREMENT PRIMARY KEY,
  name VARCHAR(50) NOT NULL,
```

```
    description TEXT NOT NULL,
    UNIQUE INDEX unq_name (name)
)
    DEFAULT CHARACTER SET utf8
    ENGINE = InnoDB;
```

Of course, this table will not be useful unless we also have a way to associate each product to one category. To do this, we will create a new column in the `product` table, which contains the id of the category that it refers to:

```
ALTER TABLE product
    ADD COLUMN category SMALLINT UNSIGNED NOT NULL;
```

Until now, all products in the `product` table are `T-shirts`. So, we can create a proper category, and associate all products to it:

```
INSERT INTO product_category
    SET name = 'T-Shirts', description = '';
UPDATE product SET category = LAST_INSERT_ID();
```

We used two simple statements here. However, the `LAST_INSERT_ID()` function is worth noting. This function returns the last `AUTO_INCREMENT` value that has been generated by the current session. It is very useful when we deal with correlated tables, as demonstrated by the preceding example. In fact, without `LAST_INSERT_ID()`, we would need to perform more statements, as follows:

1. Insert a new category.
2. Read the automatically generated ID of the new row.
3. Update the rows in `product`.

> MariaDB evaluates the result of `LAST_INSERT_ID()` before executing the SQL statement. This means that it can be safely used in a multi-row `INSERT`: its value will not change each time a new row is inserted.

Foreign keys explained

Now that we have created a relationship between `product` and `product_category`, we need a database object that enforces some rules so that we can be sure that data in these tables is always consistent. The object that we need is a foreign key.

We can think of the foreign key as a sort of link between two tables: a parent table and a child table. More specifically, it links a column in the parent table with a column in the child table (or rarely, two sets of columns). The foreign key is on the child table, and it usually references the parent table's primary key, or at least a unique index. This column is often called the **referenced column**.

Two rows are said to be **matching rows** if the value in the foreign key column matches the value in the referenced column. Sometimes, the terms parent row and child rows are also used. A parent row can have zero or more child rows. A child row can normally have only one parent row. But if a row in the child table has a NULL value in the foreign key column, it has no parent rows. In this case, it is said to be an **orphan row**.

 In MariaDB, foreign keys are only available if they are implemented by the storage engine in use. Currently, only InnoDB supports them.

In our case, the parent table is `product_category`, and the child table is `product`. The foreign key will be category, and it will reference the column `id` in `product_category`. Note that these column definitions are identical. While some differences are allowed by InnoDB, they are at the least illogical. Moreover, they can lead to frequent conversions between the different data types during the execution of SQL statements.

Before defining our first foreign key, we need to know which rules are enforced by InnoDB to guarantee data consistency. These rules are enforced when an event could potentially break the data integrity. In this case, InnoDB performs a check and, if necessary, takes action to preserve the integrity of the data. The following table shows these rules in detail:

Event	Rule
DROP TABLE on the parent table	The statement fails with an error
INSERT of a non-matching row in the child table	The insertion fails with an error
DELETE of a row in the parent table that has matches in the child table	An action chosen by the user is performed
UPDATE of a row in the parent table which modifies the value of the referenced column	An action chosen by the user is performed

As the table shows, when a DELETE or an UPDATE statement occurs on the parent table, the action performed by InnoDB is chosen by the user during foreign key creation. The possible actions are:

Action name	Description
RESTRICT or NO ACTION (default)	The operation fails with an error
CASCADE	The operation is propagated to the child table: rows are deleted, or a column value changes
SET NULL	The foreign key's column in the child table is set to NULL for the relevant rows

Users of other DBMSs will probably notice two quirks of MariaDB. The SET DEFAULT clause is accepted; that is, it does not cause any error. However, it is not implemented; so, RESTRICT will be used instead. Moreover, RESTRICT and NO ACTION are different actions for the SQL standard: the difference lies in performing the integrity checks at different stages, but this feature is not implemented in MariaDB. All checks (including checks for uniqueness) are performed immediately, and temporary inconsistencies are never allowed.

In practice, RESTRICT better protects our tables from inconsistencies, because it is not possible to perform certain operations on the parent table while the child rows exist. Other actions are less restrictive, and allow us to perform any operation on the parent table without taking care of the child table. With CASCADE, the changes will automatically be propagated; so, for example, deleting a parent row will also delete the child rows. With SET NULL, some operations will turn child rows into orphan rows.

Now, let's go back to our example. We need to create a foreign key between the product and category_product tables. We will use the category and id columns. We want the deletions of the parent rows to be propagated to the child rows; updates to the id of parent rows, however, should not be allowed. So, this is the command that we need to run:

```
ALTER TABLE product
  ADD FOREIGN KEY fk1 (category)
  REFERENCES product_category (id)
  ON DELETE CASCADE
  ON UPDATE RESTRICT;
```

If we need to remove a foreign key from a table, we need to use the following syntax:

```
ALTER TABLE <table_name> DROP FOREIGN KEY <fk_name>
```

Self-referencing tables

So, now we have product categories in our database. If we have several categories, we will probably want to implement a hierarchy, where each category can be a subcategory of another category. Unless we want to have a limit of one or two levels in the hierarchy, we need to add a `parent` column that contains a pointer to the `id` of the parent category. For the categories that do not have a parent category, this column will be set to NULL. So, let's create this column:

```
ALTER TABLE product_category
  ADD COLUMN parent SMALLINT UNSIGNED DEFAULT NULL;
```

Now, if a row has a non-NULL parent value, a row with the corresponding id must exist. So, how can we guarantee the data integrity? The answer is simple: again, we need a foreign key. In fact, a foreign key can reference a column that is in the same table. In this case, the table is a self-referencing table. There is nothing wrong with this pattern: it is generally the best way to represent trees, unidirectional graphs, and hierarchies.

Let's create the foreign key:

```
ALTER TABLE product_category
  ADD FOREIGN KEY (parent)
  REFERENCES product_category (id)
  ON DELETE RESTRICT
  ON UPDATE RESTRICT;
```

Many-to-many relationships

With the relational model, which MariaDB follows mostly, there are three types of relationships between tables:

- **one-to-one**: Every row in table A is associated with zero or one row in table B
- **one-to-many**: Every row in table A is associated with zero or more rows in table B
- **many-to-many**: Each row in table A can be associated with multiple rows in B and vice versa

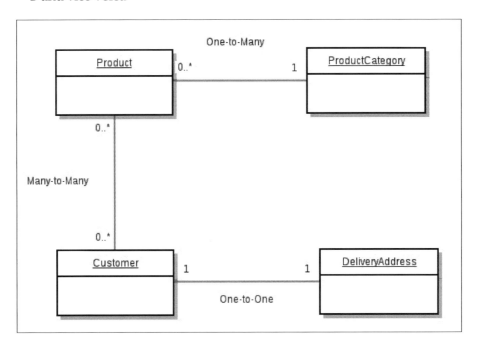

Until now, we have only used one-to-many relationships. We implemented them with a column in the child table that points to the primary key of the parent table. One-to-one relationships can be represented exactly in the same way.

However, this pattern cannot be used to represent a many-to-many relationship. With the relational model, representing a relationship of this type is a bit more complex. We need to create an auxiliary table that represents the relationship itself. This relationship table typically has only two columns pointing to the primary keys of the main tables.

A relationship table could also have other columns. For example, suppose that each product in our database can belong to more than one category. Of course, each category can (and should) contain more than one product too. So, this is a many-to-many relationship. But the relationship between a product and a category could have some properties that we need to store. For example, each product could have only one main category, shown in the product web page, and all the other categories could be considered as secondary. Similarly, each category could have one or more main products that are somehow highlighted in the catalog. So, let's remove the existing foreign key between `product` and `product_category`, and create a many-to-many relationship:

```
ALTER TABLE product DROP FOREIGN KEY fk1;

CREATE TABLE rel_product_category

(

  product INT UNSIGNED NOT NULL COMMENT 'link to product id',

  category SMALLINT UNSIGNED NOT NULL COMMENT 'link to category id',

  is_main_category TINYINT NOT NULL COMMENT 'main category for this
product?',

  is_main_product TINYINT NOT NULL COMMENT 'is product highlighted in
this category?',

  FOREIGN KEY rel_product (product)

    REFERENCES product (id)

    ON DELETE CASCADE

    ON UPDATE CASCADE,

  FOREIGN KEY rel_category (category)

    REFERENCES product_category (id)

    ON DELETE CASCADE

    ON UPDATE CASCADE

)

  ENGINE = InnoDB;
```

Like other relationships, a many-to-many relationship can link the rows in a table with other rows in the same table. In this case, we will still need an auxiliary table, and both its foreign keys will point to the same table. This is generally done to create a graph structure where each node can have multiple parents. For example, we could decide that our product categories can be part of multiple super categories, and define the relationship in the following way:

```
CREATE TABLE product_category_graph

(

  parent SMALLINT UNSIGNED NULL,
```

```
child SMALLINT UNSIGNED NOT NULL,
FOREIGN KEY graph_cat_parent (parent)
  REFERENCES product_category (id)
  ON DELETE CASCADE
  ON UPDATE CASCADE,
FOREIGN KEY graph_cat_child (child)
  REFERENCES product_category (id)
  ON DELETE CASCADE
  ON UPDATE CASCADE
)
ENGINE = InnoDB;
```

 When creating graph structures, we must be careful to avoid unwanted circular references. That is, usually a node should not be its own ancestor or descendant. Foreign keys do not preserve us from this kind of error.

Dealing with duplicates and consistency errors

Our product table does not have any UNIQUE index. However, at least one column should contain a unique value; in fact, it would be rather uncommon to have several products with the same name. So, let's add a UNIQUE index:

```
ALTER TABLE product ADD UNIQUE INDEX unq_name (name);
```

Now that we have a UNIQUE index, we can use it as an example to discuss how we can deal with duplicates with MariaDB.

Suppose that we want to add a new product, or modify an existing product. In both cases, there is a possibility that the new product name is already in use, causing a conflict. MariaDB supports several statements to automatically handle this conflict:

Syntax	Behavior
INSERT	MariaDB will simply reject the new row with an error that informs us about the problem. If we are inserting several rows with one statement, the whole statement will fail, and no rows will be added.
INSERT IGNORE	Ignore rows that cause an error. They will not be inserted, but all other rows will be added.

Syntax	Behavior
`INSERT ... ON DUPLICATE KEY UPDATE`	Try to insert a row and, if a conflict occurs, modify one or more values in the existing rows. All other values will be preserved.
`REPLACE`	This statement has the same syntax as `INSERT`. Delete the row containing that value, if it already exists, and then add the new row. If the old row exists, all its values will be lost.
`REPLACE IGNORE`	The `IGNORE` clause is also useful for the `REPLACE` statement, because deleting the existing rows could violate a foreign key constraint.
`DELETE IGNORE`	See `REPLACE IGNORE`.
`UPDATE IGNORE`	Ignore errors if one of the values we are trying to set is a duplicate.

Note that some of these clauses also affect other error types, or have other side effects, particularly the following:

- With the `IGNORE` clause, all errors are ignored, including the errors caused by foreign key constraints.

- With `REPLACE`, rows are first deleted (if present) and then re-inserted. This means that the old `AUTO_INCREMENT` value is lost along with the values generated by `TIMESTAMP` columns on insert. Also, the actions defined for the foreign key's `ON DELETE` event will be triggered.

Reading rows

Until now, we have basically learned how to insert, modify, or delete rows. We also used queries such as the following one to verify what we've written into the tables:

```
SELECT * FROM <table_name>;
```

This is the simplest query we could write: it simply reads all the columns and rows from a table. However, normally we only need to read a subset of columns and rows. We may also need to request some additional operations on the data we extract, such as ordering or grouping. The `SELECT` statement is the most complex, and we will fully explore it in this section.

Specifying the table and column names

The basic syntax for `SELECT` is:

```
SELECT <expression_list> FROM <table_name>;
```

Until now, we have always used a n asterisk (*) as an expression list. This character means all columns. However, generally, we only need to read a subset of columns. Simply typing a single character is easier, but it will cause our database to read unnecessary data and send it to the clients. To avoid a waste of resources, we should not use this syntax. The following is an example of a column list:

```
SELECT price, quantity FROM product WHERE id = 2;
```

Instead of a column name, we may want to extract the result of an expression. For example:

```
MariaDB [eshop]> SELECT price, (price / 100) * 20 as vat FROM product
WHERE id = 2;
+-------+----------+
| price | vat      |
+-------+----------+
| 25.00 | 5.000000 |
+-------+----------+
1 row in set (0.00 sec)
```

In this example, the AS keyword introduces an alias: vat. An alias sets the name of a column in the resultset, and its use is quite common for calculated columns.

If we specify the DISTINCT option, the query will eliminate the duplicate rows from the results:

```
MariaDB [eshop]> SELECT DISTINCT price FROM product;
+-------+
| price |
+-------+
| 25.00 |
+-------+
1 row in set (0.03 sec)
```

In some cases, the SELECT statement does not read any table. The following example returns the MariaDB version:

```
SELECT VERSION();
```

```
SELECT SQRT(16);
```

`SQRT()` is a function that returns the square root of a number. Several functions are available in MariaDB, and they can be useful for performing several types of calculations on the values that are stored in our database.

 We cannot discuss all the MariaDB functions in this book, and most of them are only useful in particular cases. The full list of MariaDB functions is available in the documentation, at the following URL: `https://mariadb.com/kb/en/mariadb/documentation/functions-and-operators/`.

Aggregate functions

Regular MariaDB functions return a value for each row that is extracted. For example, if we want to get all the names of the products with only lower-case letters, we can use the following code:

```
MariaDB [eshop]> SELECT LOWER(name) FROM product;
+---------------+
| LOWER(name)   |
+---------------+
| black t-shirt |
| red t-shirt   |
+---------------+
2 rows in set (0.00 sec)
```

But there is a particular type of function called **aggregate functions**. A query with an aggregate function returns only one row. These functions return a value that is calculated based on all the rows read by the query. The most important aggregate functions are:

- `COUNT(*)`: This returns the number of rows
- `AVG(<column_name>)`: Returns an arithmetical average
- `SUM(<column_name>)`: Returns the sum of the values read
- `MIN(<column_name>)`: Returns the lowest value read
- `MAX(<column_name>)`: Returns the highest value read

For example, the following query gives us the number of rows that we have in our `product` table:

```
MariaDB [eshop]> SELECT COUNT(*), AVG(price) FROM product \G
*************************** 1. row ***************************
   COUNT(*): 2
AVG(price): 25.000000
1 row in set (0.00 sec)
```

Filtering rows

The WHERE clause is very important, because it restricts the set of rows returned by a query. It specifies a condition; only rows that match that condition will be extracted.

For example, the following query returns the name of a single product:

```
MariaDB [eshop]> SELECT name FROM product WHERE id = 1;
+---------------+
| name          |
+---------------+
| Black T-Shirt |
+---------------+
1 row in set (0.00 sec)
```

The WHERE clause can be used in combination with the aggregate functions. The following query returns the number of products whose price is lower than 30, and whose available quantity is higher than 0:

```
MariaDB [eshop]> SELECT COUNT(*) FROM product WHERE price < 30 AND
quantity > 0;
+----------+
| COUNT(*) |
+----------+
|        0 |
+----------+
1 row in set (0.00 sec)
```

AND, =, and < are operators. We used several operators in our examples, and their meaning should be quite clear. In the *Operators* section of this chapter, we will discuss the operators that can be used to build complex conditions, so we will be able to write expressive and powerful queries.

Sorting rows

It is possible to sort rows in the resultset. The order can be based on one or more rows, and it can be ascending or descending. This is done with the ORDER BY clause, which has the following syntax:

```
ORDER BY <expr> [ASC | DESC], <expr> [ASC | DESC], ...
```

`<expr>` can be any SQL expression, but it is usually the name of a column. ASC specifies that the desired order is ascending, which is the default. DESC causes the order to be descending.

For example, to alphabetically sort our products by name, we can give the following query:

```
SELECT name FROM product ORDER BY name;
```

In the following example, we will sort the results by quantity and price. The order of quantity will be descending, so we will see the products that are in higher quantities first. We will restrict the results to the products that are currently available (quantity > 0):

```
SELECT name, quantity, price FROM product
ORDER BY quantity DESC, price ASC;
```

NULL values are considered lower than any other value; so, if the order is ascending, NULLs will appear first; if the order is descending, NULLs will be the last values. However, sometimes we want NULL to be considered higher than other values. To do this, we can use a condition such as this:

```
SELECT name, price FROM product ORDER BY price IS NULL, price;
```

The expression price IS NULL returns 1 if the price is NULL; otherwise it returns 0. Thus, NULL values will appear after the other values.

Limiting the number of rows

Sometimes, we want to get just specific rows from the results. For example, we can ask MariaDB to return only the first 10 rows from a resultset:

```
SELECT name FROM product ORDER BY name LIMIT 10;
```

We can also ask MariaDB to skip some rows from the beginning of a resultset. For example, this query discards the first 50 rows, and displays the following 10 rows:

```
SELECT name FROM product ORDER BY name LIMIT 10 OFFSET 50;
```

The following alternative is also supported, and does exactly the same:

```
SELECT name FROM product ORDER BY name LIMIT 50, 10;
```

 A common pitfall is trying to use `LIMIT` to optimize the execution of a query. Note, however, that adding a `LIMIT 10` does not necessarily mean that only `10` rows are read from the table. If an `ORDER BY` or a `GROUP BY` clause is used, MariaDB will have to read the whole table. Of course, `LIMIT` will still reduce the client/server communication.

`ORDER BY` and `LIMIT` can be used with the `DELETE` and `UPDATE` statements. This is useful if we have to modify or delete a large number of rows, but in smaller chunks. For example:

```
DELETE FROM product WHERE quantity = 0 ORDER BY id LIMIT 100000;
```

Grouping results

When we use an aggregate function, we always obtain a value that is calculated on a group of rows. Sometimes, this group consists of the whole table. For example, consider the following query:

```
SELECT AVG(price) FROM product;
```

We are requesting an aggregated value (the arithmetical average) from a group of rows that is the whole `product` table.

We can also divide the resultset into smaller groups, and obtain an aggregated value for each group. For example, we may want to obtain the average price for each category of the products. Each category will be a different group. The following example shows how to do this:

```
SELECT r.category, AVG(price)
  FROM product p
  LEFT JOIN rel_product_category r
    ON p.id = r.product
  GROUP BY r.category;
```

In the preceding query, we are joining two tables: in fact, the `product` table alone does not contain any information about the category. This technique will be discussed in the *Joining tables* section, but it is not important now. Just look at the `GROUP BY` clause. It contains the name of the column that is used to separate the resultset into different groups: each unique value represents a different group. And for each group, we get the average price.

Grouping can be based on any SQL expression, or even more than one expression. While simple column names are the most common type of grouping expression, it might be necessary to use some calculations.

For example, we could divide our groups further. Suppose we want to separate the products that cost less than `100` from the others even if they belong to the same category. We can do this in the following way:

```
SELECT r.category, price < 100, COUNT(*)
  FROM product p
  LEFT JOIN rel_product_category r
    ON p.id = r.product
  GROUP BY r.category, price < 100;
```

The expression `price < 100` returns `1` for prices less than `100`, and `0` for the others. This value is returned to the client, and is also used for grouping.

Joining tables

While examining the `GROUP BY` clause, we joined two tables into one resultset. This is a common operation when working with relational databases, because a table is generally correlated with other tables. The statement that allows us to do so is `JOIN`.

There are several types of joins:

- `CROSS JOIN`
- `INNER JOIN`
- `LEFT JOIN`
- `RIGHT JOIN`

The cross join operation

A `CROSS JOIN` is an operation that associates all the rows from the left table to all the rows in the right table. The number of rows in the resultset is the product of the number of rows in the left table multiplied by the number of rows in the second table, which is usually a huge number. This operation is very rarely used, and it is very expensive.

The following is an example of CROSS JOIN. Imagine we have two tables, both containing the numbers from 1 to 3:

```
MariaDB [test]> SELECT a.c, b.c FROM t1 a CROSS JOIN t2 b;
+------+------+
| c    | c    |
+------+------+
|    1 |    1 |
|    2 |    1 |
|    3 |    1 |
|    1 |    2 |
|    2 |    2 |
|    3 |    2 |
|    1 |    3 |
|    2 |    3 |
|    3 |    3 |
+------+------+
9 rows in set (0.00 sec)
```

In the preceding query, we can notice some details about the JOIN syntax. The JOIN clause always follows the FROM clause. Each table in a JOIN should have an alias: in this case the alias of t1 is a, and the alias of t2 is b. Aliases prevent ambiguities if the tables have some columns with the same names.

The CROSS keyword is optional.

The inner join operation

While CROSS JOIN associates all the rows in a table with all rows in another table, other JOIN types selectively associate only some rows from the two tables. A join condition specifies the rows that will be associated.

An INNER JOIN, also known as a simple join, only returns the associated rows.

Consider the following example:

```
SELECT p.id, c.id
  FROM product p
  INNER JOIN rel_product_category r
```

```
   ON p.id = r.product
INNER JOIN product_category c
   ON r.category = c.id
WHERE p.price > 500;
```

In the preceding example, we are extracting the IDs of the products whose price is higher than 500, and the IDs of their categories.

We are joining two tables. A JOIN clause is specified for each table to be joined.

The ON clauses specify the join conditions. These conditions are very simple: we are just checking that the two values match. On rare occasions, we may want to use complex join conditions, such as the ones we used when discussing the WHERE clause. This is sometimes done to optimize query execution, but this topic is beyond the scope of this book.

Since the ON clauses are present, the INNER keyword is unnecessary: it is the default join type.

The left join and right join operations

LEFT JOIN and RIGHT JOIN are collectively known as **outer joins**.

A LEFT JOIN extracts all the rows from the left table and, when possible, associates them to the rows that match the join condition in the right table. The rows from the left table that don't have any associations will have the values of the right table columns set to NULL.

A RIGHT JOIN operates in an opposite fashion: it extracts all the rows from the right table, and only some rows from the left table. It can be useful when joining several tables, but it is rarely used.

 Some relational DBMSs also support a third outer join type: FULL OUTER JOIN. It returns the associated rows, along with the unassociated rows from both the tables. This operation is not supported in MariaDB and, anyway, it does not have many practical uses.

The following is an example of a LEFT JOIN:

```
MariaDB [eshop]> SELECT c.id, c.name, r.product
    -> FROM product_category c
    -> LEFT JOIN rel_product_category r
    -> ON c.id = r.category
```

```
    -> WHERE r.product IS NULL;
+----+--------+---------+
| id | name   | product |
+----+--------+---------+
| 15 | Hats   |    NULL |
| 16 | Scarfs |    NULL |
| 10 | Shoes  |    NULL |
+----+--------+---------+
3 rows in set (0.00 sec)
```

In the preceding example, we are interested in the categories that have no associated products, or empty categories. We use a LEFT JOIN because this join type also returns the rows in the left table (product_category) that have no matching rows in the right table. Then, we only extract the rows without any associations by discarding the rows having a product value other than NULL.

All the SQL JOIN operations can be summarized with the following diagram:

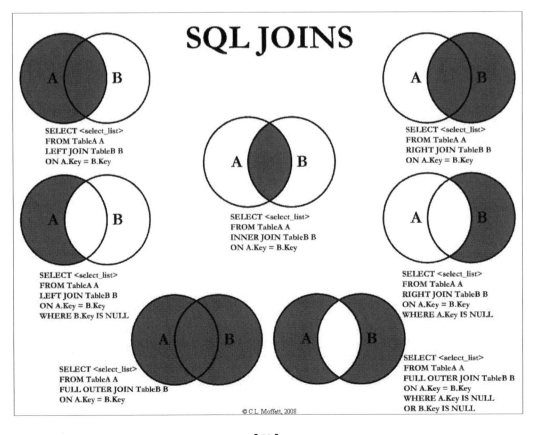

Unions

Sometimes, we have tables that represent similar entities—for example, customers and suppliers. Such tables can have some identical columns—for example `first_name`, `last_name`, `email`, and `phone`. Say, for some reason, we want to keep these entities separated, but, in some situations, we would like to get results from both the tables with one statement. (For example, we may want to have a list of suppliers and customer e-mail addresses and phone numbers). We can do this in the following way:

```
(SELECT first_name, last_name, email, phone FROM suppliers)
UNION
(SELECT first_name, last_name, email, phone FROM customer);
```

The `UNION` statement merges two or more resultsets into one. There is, of course, a restriction: these resultsets must have the same columns, in the same order.

Now suppose that some of our suppliers are also our customers. Suppose that we do not want them to appear twice in the result set. For this reason, MariaDB, by default, eliminates the duplicate rows from the `UNION`'s results. But if we want to preserve duplicates, we can use the `ALL` keyword:

```
(SELECT first_name, last_name, email, phone FROM suppliers)
UNION ALL
(SELECT first_name, last_name, email, phone FROM customer);
```

The `UNION` statement also supports the `ORDER BY` and `LIMIT` clauses:

```
(SELECT first_name, last_name, email, phone FROM suppliers)
UNION ALL
(SELECT first_name, last_name, email, phone FROM customer)
ORDER BY last_name LIMIT 100;
```

> The inner `SELECT` queries can have the `ORDER BY` and `LIMIT` clauses, too. However, it is important to remember that these clauses only apply to the query they belong to and not to the `UNION`'s resultset. In general, an `ORDER BY` without `LIMIT` is useless in an inner `SELECT`, because it does not determine the order of `UNION`'s results.

Subqueries

A **subquery** is a `SELECT` query that is nested in another statement. The outer statement can be any of `SELECT`, `INSERT`, `REPLACE`, `UPDATE`, or `DELETE`.

Scalar subqueries

The simplest subquery type is called a **scalar subquery**. It is a subquery that returns a single value. A scalar subquery can be used whenever an SQL expression is allowed.

Consider the following example:

```
UPDATE product SET quantity = quantity - (
    SELECT SUM(quantity) FROM `order` WHERE product = 2
) WHERE id = 2;
```

The UPDATE statement subtracts a certain number from the quantity field of a certain product. The value to be subtracted is the sum of the ordered products, and is calculated by the subquery.

If a scalar subquery returns no rows, it results in a NULL value.

Row subqueries

A **row subquery** is a subquery that returns multiple values in a single row. This type of subquery requires a particular syntax, as shown in the following example:

```
SELECT id, name FROM `order` WHERE (price, quantity) =
(SELECT price, quantity FROM product WHERE id = 2);
```

The special syntax used in the WHERE clause is required, because we want to compare two columns with the two values returned by the subquery.

This syntactic element is called a **row constructor**. It can be used even without subqueries, as shown in the following example:

```
SELECT id, name FROM `order` WHERE (price, quantity) = (100, 20);
```

A row subquery must always return one row. If it returns multiple rows, or no rows, an error is issued.

Table subqueries

A **table subquery** is a subquery that, returns multiple rows. It is not possible to use a table subquery with normal operators that are used with other subqueries. For example, we cannot compare the results of two table subqueries with the equal to operator (=). The following example shows that, in this case, we would see an error:

```
MariaDB [eshop]> SELECT (SELECT id FROM product) > 1;
ERROR 1242 (21000): Subquery returns more than 1 row
```

In fact, such a comparison would not make sense. The following operators are designed to work with table subqueries:

Operator	Description
EXISTS <subquery>	Returns 1 if subquery returns at least one row.
NOT EXISTS <subquery>	Returns 1 if subquery returns no rows.
<value> IN <subquery>	Returns 1 if value is contained in subquery.
<value> NOT IN <subquery>	Returns 1 if value is not contained in subquery, or subquery returns no rows.
<value> <operator> ALL <subquery>	Returns 1 if the comparison holds true for all the rows returned by subquery, or subquery returns no rows.
<value> <operator> ANY <subquery>	Returns 1 if the comparison is true for at least one row.
<value> <operator> SOME <subquery>	Synonym for ANY.

Let's see some examples:

```
SELECT id FROM product WHERE EXISTS
    (SELECT product FROM rel_product_category WHERE product = id);
```

This query extracts the products that are associated with at least one category. This is very similar to the example that we used for discussing LEFT JOIN; in fact, subqueries similar to this can generally be rewritten as joins. MariaDB usually rewrites these queries internally to optimize the execution time.

```
MariaDB [eshop]> SELECT (25, 0) IN (SELECT price, quantity FROM product);
+---------------------------------------------------+
| (25, 0) IN (SELECT price, quantity FROM product)  |
+---------------------------------------------------+
|                                                 1 |
+---------------------------------------------------+
1 row in set (0.01 sec)
```

The preceding example shows that if a table query returns more than one column, a row constructor must be used to compare the results. In this case, we use IN to check if at least one row has a price of 25 and a quantity of 0.

```
MariaDB [eshop]> SELECT 1 < ANY (SELECT id FROM product);
+-----------------------------------+
| 1 < ANY (SELECT id FROM product)  |
```

```
+----------------------------------+
|                              1 |
+----------------------------------+
1 row in set (0.00 sec)


MariaDB [eshop]> SELECT 1 < ALL (SELECT id FROM product);
+----------------------------------+
| 1 < ALL (SELECT id FROM product) |
+----------------------------------+
|                              0 |
+----------------------------------+
1 row in set (0.00 sec)
```

The preceding example shows the difference between ANY and ALL. Since product has rows with id higher than 1, the first query returns 1. But since a row exists with an id of 1, the second query returns 0.

Derived tables

A **derived table** is a subquery that is used in the FROM clause of a SELECT statement. Its results are used as if they were a real table. A derived table must always have an alias. The following example shows the syntax:

```
SELECT SUM(num) FROM (
    (SELECT COUNT(*) AS num FROM supplier)
    UNION
    (SELECT COUNT(*) AS num FROM customer)
) dt;
```

In this example, MariaDB will execute the derived table first. It will return two rows containing the number of rows in supplier, and the number of rows in customer. Then, the outer SELECT will return a sum of these rows. There is no other way to obtain this particular result with a single query in MariaDB. However, in most cases, the use of a derived table is not necessary. Keep in mind that a query using a derived table often results in a less-than-optimal execution time.

Working with operators

In our examples, we used several operators, such as equals (=), less than, and greater than (<, >), and others. Now it is time to discuss operators in general, and list the most important ones.

In general, an operator is a sign that takes one or more operands, and returns a result. Several groups of operators exist in MariaDB. In this section, we will discuss the main types:

- Comparison operators
- String operators
- Logical operators
- Arithmetic operators

Comparison operators

A comparison operator checks if there is a certain relationship between its operands. If the relationship exists, the operator returns 1; otherwise it returns 0. For example, let's take the `equality` operator, which is probably the most used:

```
1 = 1 -- returns 1: the equality relationship exists
1 = 0 -- returns 0: no equality relationship here
```

In MariaDB, 1 and 0 are used in many contexts to indicate if something is `true` or `false`. In fact, MariaDB does not have a Boolean data type, so TRUE and FALSE are merely used as aliases for 1 and 0:

```
TRUE = 1 -- returns 1
FALSE = 0 -- returns 1
TRUE = FALSE -- returns 0
```

In a WHERE clause, a result of 0 or NULL prevents a row from being shown. All numeric results other than 0, including negative numbers, are regarded as true in this context. Non-numeric values other than NULL need to be converted into numbers in order to be evaluated by the WHERE clause. Non-numeric strings are converted to 0; numeric strings are treated as numbers. Dates are converted to non-zero numbers.

```
WHERE 1 -- is redundant; it shows all the rows
WHERE 0 -- prevents all the rows from being shown
```

Now, let's take a look at the MariaDB comparison operators:

Operator	Description	Example
=	Equality	A = B
!=	Inequality	A != B
<>	Synonym for !=	A <> B
<	Less than	A < B
>	Greater than	A > B
<=	Less than or equal to	A <= B
>=	Greater than or equal to	A >= B
IS NULL	The operand is NULL	A IS NULL
IS NOT NULL	The operand is not NULL	A IS NOT NULL
<=>	The operands are equal, or they both are NULL	A <=> B
BETWEEN ... AND	The left operand is within a range of values	A BETWEEN B AND C
NOT BETWEEN ... AND	The left operand is outside the specified range	A NOT BETWEEN B AND C
IN	The left operand is one of the items in a given list	A IN (B, C, D)
NOT IN	The left operand is not in the given list	A NOT IN (B, C, D)

A couple of examples are as follows:

```
SELECT id FROM product WHERE price BETWEEN 100 AND 200;
DELETE FROM product WHERE id IN (100, 101, 102);
```

Special attention should be paid to the NULL values. Almost all the previously listed operators return NULL if any of their operands are NULL. The reason is quite clear: since NULL represents an unknown value, any operation involving a NULL operand returns an unknown result.

There are, however, some operators specifically designed to work with the NULL values. IS NULL and IS NOT NULL test whether the operand is NULL. The <=> operator is a shortcut for:

```
a = b OR (a IS NULL AND b IS NULL)
```

String operators

MariaDB supports some comparison operators that are specifically designed to work with string values. This does not mean that other operators do not work well with strings. For example, A = B works perfectly if A and B are strings. However, some specific comparisons only make sense with text values. Let's take a look at them.

The LIKE operator and its variants

This operator is often used to check if a string starts with a given sequence of characters, if it ends with that sequence, or if it contains the sequence. More generally, LIKE checks if a string follows a given pattern. Its syntax is:

```
<string_value> LIKE <pattern>
```

The pattern is a string that can contain the following wildcard characters:

- _ (underscore), which means any character
- %, which means any sequence of 0 or more characters

There is also a way to include these characters without their special meaning: the _ and \% sequences represent the characters _ and % respectively.

For example, take the following expressions:

```
my_text LIKE 'h_'
my_text LIKE 'h%'
```

The first expression returns 1 for 'hi', 'ha', or 'ho', but not for 'hey'. The second expression returns 1 for all these strings, including 'hey'.

By default, LIKE is case-insensitive, which means that 'abc' LIKE 'ABC' returns 1. Thus, it can be used to perform a case-insensitive equality check. To make LIKE case-insensitive, the BINARY keyword can be used as follows:

```
my_text LIKE BINARY your_text
```

The complement of LIKE is NOT LIKE:

```
<string_value> NOT LIKE <pattern>
```

The following are the most common uses for LIKE:

```
my_text LIKE 'my%' -- does my_text start with 'my'?
my_text LIKE '%my' -- does my_text end with 'my'?
my_text LIKE '%my%' -- does my_text contain 'my'?
```

More complex uses are possible for LIKE. For example, the following expression can be used to check if `mail` is a valid e-mail address:

```
mail LIKE '_%@_%._ _%'
```

The preceding snippet checks if `mail` contains, in this order, at least one character, a `'@'` character, at least one character, a dot, at least two characters. In most cases, an invalid e-mail address will not pass this test.

Using regular expressions with the REGEXP operator and its variants

Regular expressions are string patterns containing a metacharacter with special meaning to perform match operations, and to determine if a given string matches the given pattern or not.

The REGEXP operator is somewhat similar to LIKE: it checks whether a string matches a given pattern. However, REGEXP uses regular expressions, with the syntax defined by the POSIX standard. Basically, this means that:

- Many developers, but not all, already know their syntax
- REGEXP uses a very expressive syntax, so the patterns can be much more complex and detailed
- REGEXP is much slower than LIKE, which should be preferred when possible

> Regular expression syntax is a complex topic, and it cannot be covered in this book. Developers can learn about regular expressions from www.regular-expressions.info.

The complement of REGEXP is NOT REGEXP.

Logical operators

Logical operators can be used to combine truth expressions, thereby forming a compound expression that can be true, false, or NULL. Depending on the truth values of its operands, a logical operator can return 1 or 0.

MariaDB supports the following logical operators:

- NOT
- AND
- OR
- XOR

The NOT operator

NOT is the only logical operator that takes one operand. It inverts its truth value. If the operand is true, NOT returns 0; if the operand is false, NOT returns 1. If the operand is NULL, NOT returns NULL.

For example:

```
NOT 1 -- returns 0
NOT 0 -- returns 1
NOT 1 = 1 -- returns 0
NOT 1 = NULL -- returns NULL
NOT 1 <=> NULL -- returns 0
```

The AND operator

AND returns 1 if both its operands are true, and 0 in all other cases. For example:

```
1 AND 1 -- returns 1
0 AND 1 -- returns 0
0 AND 0 -- returns 0
```

The OR operator

OR returns 1 if at least one of its operators is true, or 0 if both the operators are false. For example:

```
1 OR 1 -- returns 1
0 OR 1 -- returns 1
0 OR 0 -- returns 0
```

The XOR operator

XOR stands for **eXclusive OR**. It is the least-used logical operator. It returns 1 if only one of its operators is true, or 0 if both the operands are true or false. For example:

```
1 XOR 1 -- returns 0
1 XOR 0 -- returns 1
0 XOR 1 --returns 1
0 XOR 0 -- returns 0
```

A XOR B is the equivalent of the following expression:

```
(A OR B) AND NOT (A AND B)
```

Or:

```
(NOT A AND B) OR (A AND NOT B)
```

Arithmetic operators

MariaDB supports the operators that are necessary to execute all the basic arithmetical operations. The supported arithmetic operators are:

- + for addition
- - for subtraction
- * for multiplication
- / for division

 Remember that a division by 0 raises an error or returns NULL, depending on the MariaDB configuration.

In addition, two more operators are useful for division:

- DIV returns the integer part of a division, without any decimal part or remainder
- MOD, or %, returns the remainder of a division operation

For example:

```
MariaDB [(none)]> SELECT 20 DIV 3 AS int_part, 20 MOD 3 AS modulus;
+----------+---------+
| int_part | modulus |
+----------+---------+
|        6 |       2 |
+----------+---------+
1 row in set (0.00 sec)
```

Operator precedence

MariaDB does not blindly evaluate the expression from left to right. Every operator has a given precedence. The And operator, which is evaluated before any of the others, is said to have a higher precedence.

In general, arithmetic and string operators have a higher priority than logical operators. The precedence of the arithmetic operators reflects their precedence in common mathematical expressions. It is very important to remember the precedence of the logical operators, from the highest to the lowest:

- NOT
- AND
- XOR
- OR

> MariaDB supports many operators, but we will not discuss all of them. Also, the exact precedence can vary slightly depending on the MariaDB configuration. The complete precedence order can be found in the MariaDB Knowledge Base, at the following URL: https://mariadb.com/kb/en/mariadb/documentation/functions-and-operators/operator-precedence/.

Parentheses can be used to force MariaDB to follow a certain order. They are also useful when we do not remember the exact precedence of the operators that we are using:

```
(NOT (a AND b)) OR c OR d
```

Working with times and dates

As we discussed in *Chapter 2*, *Databases and Tables*, MariaDB supports the following temporal data types:

- DATE
- TIME
- DATETIME
- TIMESTAMP

Working with this kind of data requires specifically-designed functions and syntaxes. This section discusses how to perform the most common temporal operations.

Writing temporal values

With old MariaDB versions, DATE, TIME, and DATETIME values can only be written as strings. This syntax has been designed to be as error-proof as possible, which makes it very easy to use. Some examples are as follows:

- '1994-01-01'
- '1994-01-01 12:30:00'
- '12:30'

Starting from version 10.0, the standard SQL syntax can be used. This eliminates ambiguities in the rare cases when MariaDB does not know if a value should be regarded as a string or as a date. The standard syntax is:

- DATE '1994-01-01'
- TIMESTAMP '1994-01-01 12:30:00'
- TIME '12:30'

Adding and subtracting time intervals

It is possible to add or subtract a time interval to specific temporal data. The syntax to do this is the following:

```
<temporal_value> {+ | -} INTERVAL <number> <time_unit>
```

For example, to select the next day's date, we can use the following syntax:

```
MariaDB [(none)]> SELECT NOW() + INTERVAL 1 DAY;
+------------------------+
| NOW() + INTERVAL 1 DAY |
+------------------------+
| 2014-11-10 22:05:59    |
+------------------------+
1 row in set (0.00 sec)
```

A more common example is that of extracting the list of adults from a table:

```
SELECT id FROM users WHERE birth_date > (NOW() - INTERVAL 21 YEAR);
```

Extracting date or time parts

Very often, we want to extract a single time or part of a date from a temporal value. For example, if we have the birth dates of a few people in a table, we may want to know how many of them were born in a given year. In this case, we will use the YEAR() function, which extracts the year part from a temporal value:

```
SELECT COUNT(*) FROM users WHERE YEAR(birth_date) = 2000;
```

MariaDB provides a function for any time unit we may want to extract from a temporal value. These functions are listed here, from the smallest to the greatest time unit:

- MICROSECOND()
- SECOND()
- MINUTE()
- HOUR()
- DAY()
- DAYOFWEEK(), returns a result from 0 to 6
- DAYOFMONTH(), returns a result from 1 to 31
- DAYOFYEAR(), returns a result from 0 to 366
- WEEKOFYEAR(), returns a result from 1 to 53
- MONTH()
- QUARTER()
- YEAR()

Using comments to annotate your database schema

Comments are annotations that users can write in their queries or in their batch files. MariaDB ignores them.

Two different syntaxes can be used to write one-line comments:

```
SELECT 1 # why are we doing this?
AS uno -- this is the Italian word for one!
;
```

When the parsers finds a # character or a -- sequence, it ignores the rest of the line. Note, however, that the -- characters should be followed by a space character. If there are no spaces, they are considered as two arithmetic operators.

Sometimes, we want to write comments that spread over more than one line. Of course, it is possible to start each line with the # character or the – sequence. But we may prefer to use the specific multi-line syntax:

```
SELECT
/*
  This is a multi-line comment.
  The indentation is not necessary,
  but it can make the comment more readable.
*/
version();
```

 Note that multi-line comments cannot be nested.

Executable comments

We stated earlier that comments are ignored by the parser. This is not entirely true: a special class of comments, called `executable comments`, are ignored by certain versions of MariaDB and MySQL, and executed by other versions.

Executable comments are very useful if we want to use certain features that were introduced in some recent versions of MariaDB, and still be able to execute the same queries with the older MariaDB versions. Similarly, we may want to use some MariaDB features that are not present in MySQL, and still be able to execute the queries on MySQL.

A comment starting with /*! will only be executed on MariaDB and MySQL, but not on other DBMSs. In fact, we may want to write queries once, and execute them on MariaDB, MySQL, or any other database server that supports standard SQL. With this feature, we will still be able to use the non-standard features of MariaDB and MySQL.

For example:

```
CREATE TABLE tab_name
(
  ...
)
  /*! ENGINE = InnoDB */;
```

This example executes the non-standard clause ENGINE on MariaDB and MySQL, but not on other DBMSs.

Adding an M letter, we can write a comment that is executed only on MariaDB, and not by MySQL:

```
CREATE TABLE tab_name
(
  ...
  /*M! virtual_column VARCHAR(5) AS (left(b,5)) PERSISTENT */
)
  ENGINE = InnoDB;
```

To make old versions of MariaDB and MySQL ignore a portion of a statement, we must include it in an executable comment, and specify the lowest MariaDB version that should execute the statement. The syntax to do this is the following:

```
/*!NNNNNN <some_sql> */
```

The NNNNNN placeholder represents a sequence of six digits representing a MariaDB/MySQL version. This information is structured as follows:

- The first two digits (optionally, only one) represent the major version
- The following two digits represent the minor version
- The final two digits represent the patch version

In many cases, we will use 00 as the patch version, because it is not really relevant.

Lastly, we can add an M and also specify a version number. This makes a comment executable only on recent versions of MariaDB.

For example, the following executable comment will be ignored by versions of MariaDB that are older than version 10.0:

```
CREATE /*M!100000 OR REPLACE */ TABLE tab_name ... ;
```

Summary

In this chapter, we discussed most of the SQL statements and features that are normally used when working with a database.

First, we discussed the statements that are used to modify data: INSERT, UPDATE, REPLACE, and DELETE. Then we learned the basis of transactions, a mechanism used to isolate the operations performed by different connections to avoid conflicts between them. We also examined foreign keys, a way to guarantee data integrity and automate some operations on correlated tables.

Then, we discussed the statements used to query data: simple SELECT, JOIN, UNION, and finally, subqueries.

Furthermore, we examined the most commonly used MariaDB operators that are needed to write or read data. We also learned how to perform some common operations on temporal values.

In the last section, we discussed comments. While comments are commonly seen as a way to write annotations in the code, MariaDB and MySQL support what they call executable comments. Thanks to this feature, we can use specific features of MySQL, MariaDB, or even recent versions of MariaDB, in queries that will still work on other database systems.

In the next chapter, we will learn how to import data into MariaDB, and how to export data and perform backups.

4
Importing and Exporting Data

In the previous chapters, we learned how to install MariaDB, create our databases and tables, and how to work with our data. Even if we're yet to learn many of the interesting features of MariaDB, we are now ready to use it for our day-to-day work. However, there is still something that we definitely need to know: *how to import and export data*. We will learn this topic in the present chapter.

In this chapter, we will discuss the following topics:

- The basics of importing and exporting data
- Creating and importing CSV files
- Creating and running a dump file
- Making the restore of a database faster

The basics of importing and exporting data

There are several reasons for importing data into MariaDB, or for exporting data from it. The most common reason is taking a backup. In most databases, the data changes frequently. This means that a backup becomes old very quickly. For this reason, we should back up our important data regularly as well as frequently. If data gets lost for any reason, like due to a server crash or due to a bug in an application, we will need to import our backup.

Note that taking a backup before doing something that involves any risk is very important too. For example, we should always take a backup before upgrading our MariaDB version, or before replacing MySQL with MariaDB. It is very unlikely that such operations will cause any damage, but in case it happens we would like to be ready.

We could also export our data to import it into another server, or distribute it as part of an application. It need not be a MariaDB server; it could be MySQL or, in many cases, it could be another DBMS, such as PostgreSQL or FirebirdSQL. And, of course, we can import data that has been exported from another DBMS as well.

Depending on our purpose and other considerations, we can choose from several methods for exporting data. In this chapter, we will examine the following methods:

- CSV files created and imported with SQL statements
- Dump files created with the `mysqldump` tool

Creating and importing CSV files

CSV is the most common file format used for data interchange. CSV files are readable by a human being, so they can be examined or modified with a simple text editor, like vim or gedit on Linux, or Notepad++ on Windows. The format rules are very simple, so it is also very easy to write a script that reads, writes, or modifies the CSV data. Among the human-readable data formats, CSV is the least verbose, which makes it suitable for non-trivial amounts of data.

There are other, human-readable formats such as JSON or XML, as well. They are much more flexible than CSV: they can be used to store any type of data, including trees, graphs, and non-structured information. Because of this characteristic, they require more space, and parsing them requires more complex programs. CSV has been designed for tabular data, which makes it optimal when we need to interchange or back-up relational databases.

CSV stands for Comma Separated Values. A CSV file always consists of a series of rows that contain one or more values. Many variants of this format exist, and each variant uses different separators and special characters. Here we will describe the most commonly used characters:

- Individual values are separated by a comma (,)
- Text data is optionally enclosed with in double quotes ("), so they can contain commas
- Quoted texts can also contain double quotes, which must be escaped with a backslash (\ )
- A double backslash in a quoted text represents a single backslash character
- Rows are usually separated by a new line character (\n); sometimes they are separated by the typical Windows character sequence: a line feed followed by a new line (\r\n)

The following is a small example:

```
1,"Black T-Shirt",25.00,0,""
2,"Red T-Shirt",25.00,0,""
```

The first line of a CSV file can optionally be a list of columns names, separated by a comma. This often makes the files easier to read and parse.

MariaDB supports three ways to write or read a CSV file:

- The CSV storage engine
- The CONNECT storage engine
- The SQL statements SELECT ... INTO OUTFILE and LOAD DATA INFILE

The CSV storage engine is very useful in MySQL, but it has several limitations; so, there are not many reasons to use it on modern MariaDB versions. We will not discuss the CSV engine in this book.

Since MariaDB 10.0, the CONNECT storage engine is certainly the best way to work with most types of external data source, including CSV files. We will discuss it in *Chapter 8, Using the CONNECT Storage Engine*.

SQL statements that write and read CSV files have at least four important advantages:

- They support NULL values, which are not supported by CSV and only partially supported by CONNECT
- A CSV file can be populated with filtered and transformed table contents
- They allow importing of data into a table or exporting data from a table with only one command
- They work perfectly on older MariaDB versions, on MariaDB installations that do not have CONNECT, and on MySQL

In the following subsections, we will discuss these statements.

 Note that these statements require the FILE privilege. Normally, it is only assigned to root.

The SELECT ... INTO OUTFILE statement

The SELECT statement has an INTO OUTFILE optional clause. When this clause is used, the query's output is written into a CSV file, and is not sent to the client.

Normal SELECT clauses, such as WHERE and ORDER BY, are allowed with SELECT ... INTO OUTFILE. However, it has several optional clauses affecting the format of the CSV file. Let's see the complete syntax:

```
SELECT
   [normal_select_syntax]
   INTO OUTFILE 'file_name'
[CHARACTER SET charset_name]
   [{FIELDS | COLUMNS}
     [TERMINATED BY 'string']
     [[OPTIONALLY] ENCLOSED BY 'char']
     [ESCAPED BY 'char']
   ]
   [LINES
     [STARTING BY 'string']
     [TERMINATED BY 'string']
   ]
```

Most of these clauses are also used with LOAD DATA INFILE. This allows us to use LOAD DATA INFILE for importing any CSV file that was created with SELECT ... INTO OUTFILE.

Let's see these clauses in detail.

File options

The file name must be enclosed by quotes like any SQL string. It can include a relative or absolute path. Relative paths start from the MariaDB data directory, which is indicated in the @@datadir server variable. If no path is specified and a default database is selected, the file will be placed in the database directory, which is a subdirectory of the data directory.

Note that MariaDB needs to have write permissions on the target directory. Moreover, be aware that SELECT ... INTO OUTFILE never overwrites existing files; if the target file exists, the following error is produced:

```
MariaDB [eshop]> SELECT * FROM product INTO OUTFILE
'/tmp/product.csv';ERROR 1086 (HY000): File '/tmp/product.csv'
already exists
```

All other clauses are optional.

By default, the CSV file will be encoded in the character set specified in the `@@character_set_filesystem` server variable. To use a different character set, we can use the CHARACTER SET clause, as shown in the following example:

```
SELECT * FROM product
  INTO OUTFILE '/tmp/product.csv'
  CHARACTER SET utf8;
```

Column options

Column options define the way in which the individual values are written. The COLUMNS or FIELDS keyword must be specified only once, before all column options. FIELDS is just a synonym for COLUMNS that can be used in several MariaDB statements.

The following options are supported:

Option syntax	Description	Default value
TERMINATED BY 'string'	Character or sequence of characters used as a separator.	Horizontal tab ('\t').
[OPTIONALLY] ENCLOSED BY 'char'	Character used to quote values. If OPTIONALLY is specified, only strings will be quoted.	Empty string.
ESCAPED BY 'char'	This character will be used inside a quoted string to escape the quote character and itself.	Backslash (\).

The following example uses all the available options:

```
SELECT * FROM product
  INTO OUTFILE '/tmp/product.csv'
  COLUMNS
    TERMINATED BY ','
    ENCLOSED BY '"'
    ESCAPED BY '\\';
```

Row options

Row options affect the way rows are written to the CSV file. Similar to the column options, row options must be preceded by the `LINES` keyword, which must appear only once.

The following options are supported:

Option syntax	Description	Default value
`STARTING BY 'string'`	All lines, including the first one, will start with this string.	Empty string.
`TERMINATED BY 'string'`	All lines, including the last one, will end with this string.	New line (`'\n'`).

The following example writes a file using a semicolon (`;`) to separate values, and a double semicolon at the end of each line:

```
SELECT * FROM product
  INTO OUTFILE '/tmp/product.csv'
  COLUMNS TERMINATED BY ';'
  LINES TERMINATED BY ';;\n';
```

The LOAD DATA INFILE statement

The `LOAD DATA INFILE` statement reads the data from a CSV file, and writes it into a table. This statement has the same options as `SELECT ... INTO OUTFILE`, plus others that can be useful for importing CSV files created outside MariaDB. Moreover, `LOAD DATA INFILE` is faster than the default import.

The syntax is the following:

```
LOAD DATA [LOCAL] INFILE 'file_name' [REPLACE | IGNORE]
  INTO TABLE tbl_name
  [CHARACTER SET charset_name]
  [ column_options ]
  [ row_option ]
  [IGNORE num {LINES | ROWS}]
  [(column_name, ...)]
  [SET column_name = expr, ...]
```

Since we have already discussed many of these options, here we will explain the clauses that are used in `LOAD DATA INFILE` only.

With the LOCAL option, we declare that the file we are loading is located in the client host. If we consider this feature too risky in our situation, we can disable it by starting mysqld with the `--local-infile=0` option, or set the `@@local_infile` variable to `0`. If the LOCAL option is not used, the file is expected to be located in the server. If the client and the server are running on the same host, LOCAL is useless.

The LOAD DATA INFILE statement can deal with duplicate rows in three ways:

- By default, it simply returns an error and stops execution. For transactional tables, such as InnoDB, this means that the whole operation is rolled back. For non-transactional tables, such as MyISAM or Aria, this means that data will be partially written.
- If REPLACE is specified, the newest rows will replace the older ones.
- With IGNORE, old rows will be preserved and newer duplicates will not be loaded.

As we mentioned, the first row of a CSV file may contain the column names. Or maybe the first lines could be used for other metainformation or for comments. For example, they could contain the name of the original table, as well as a timestamp of the backup. In these cases, the first lines should be ignored by MariaDB. To achieve this, we can use the IGNORE LINES option. For example:

```
LOAD DATA INFILE 'product.csv' INTO TABLE product IGNORE 1 LINES;
```

By default, MariaDB assumes that the order of the columns is the same in the file and in the target table. If this is not the case, or if we are not sure, we have to specify the order in which the columns are written in the file. The column list must be wrapped inside parentheses, as in the following example:

```
LOAD DATA INFILE 'product.csv' INTO TABLE product
(id, name, price, quantity, description);
```

Note that it is even possible to omit some columns from the end of the rows: in this way, they will not be loaded.

The SET clause allows us to use SQL expressions to transform the values read from a file. First, we load a value into a variable instead of a column; then, we specify an expression. The following example should clarify the process:

```
LOAD DATA INFILE ...
  (col_1, @var)
  SET col_2 = @var * 100;
```

Creating and importing a dump file

A dump file, or simply a dump, is a text file containing the SQL queries that are necessary to recreate a database or all the databases in a MariaDB instance.

Dump files can be created with a tool called `mysqldump`, a tool distributed along with MariaDB. This program will be discussed in the next subsection. A dump can later be imported into MariaDB by passing it to the `mysql` command-line client. We have already discussed this technique in *Chapter 1, Installing MariaDB*, and we will not repeat it here. However, the restoring of dump files is covered in the final examples.

Dumps generated with `mysqldump` make use of executable comments for any MariaDB or MySQL-specific features. These executable comments include the version numbers for all the features introduced since the MySQL 4.1 version, which went into production in 2004. This makes it possible to load dumps into any version of MariaDB and MySQL, not necessarily a recent one. Loading them into other DBMSs is also possible, yet some small modifications could be necessary.

Using mysqldump

`mysqldump` has many options that affect its behavior. In this book, we will only discuss the most important ones. For example, we are leaving out all the options that are only useful in a replication environment, because they are not relevant for beginners.

Anyway, to get a list of available options, we can run:

```
mysqldump --help
```

> Before using `mysqldump` for a complex backup, reading its documentation page is recommended. It can be found at this URL: https://mariadb.com/kb/en/mariadb/documentation/clients-and-utilities/backup-restore-and-import/mysqldump/.

Login options

We discussed the `mysql` command-line client's login options in *Chapter 1, Installing MariaDB*. There is no need to repeat them here: those options are the same for all the MariaDB official tools.

Choosing what to dump

Depending on your project, you may have different needs. You may want to back-up one or multiple databases, or even pick only a few tables in your database.

The basic syntax of `mysqldump` depends on which objects you want to back up.

- Dumping *one or more tables*:

  ```
  mysqldump [options]<db_name> <tab_name>, <tab_name>, ...
  ```

- Dumping *one database*:

  ```
  mysqldump <db_name>
  ```

- Dumping *multiple databases*:

  ```
  mysqldump [options] --databases <db_name>, <db_name>, ...
  ```

- Dumping *all databases*:

  ```
  mysqldump [options] --all-databases
  ```

The `--no-data` option allows us to dump the structure of these objects, with no data. In this case, the dump will be able to recreate a database and its tables, but the tables will be empty.

Or we may want to only get a dump of the data, without the CREATE DATABASE and CREATE TABLE statements. The options to exclude these statements are `--no-create-db` and `--no-create-info`.

Options affecting the dumping operation

Once we have decided what we want to dump, we should use some options to affect the way `mysqldump` reads the data.

Some SQL errors may cause `mysqldump` to stop. To ignore those errors and continue the execution, we can specify the `--force` option.

To ensure data consistency amongst all tables, the `--single-transaction` option can be used. It sets the isolation level to `repeatable read`, which doesn't block queries from other sessions, and causes `mysqldump` to read all the tables within the same transaction. While this is not the default behavior, this option should normally be used.

Of course, the former option is only useful when dumping transactional tables. When dumping non-transactional tables, such a MyISAM or Aria, we should use the `--lock-tables` or `--lock-all-tables` option. The former acquires a global read lock to guarantee data integrity across all databases. The latter only locks one database at a time, thus allowing better concurrency. But it should not be used if the data contains cross-database references.

 The options `--single-transaction`, `--lock-tables`, and `--lock-all-tables` should not be used together. `mysqldump` would take into account one of them and ignore the others.

The `--quick` option causes the rows to be read and written one at a time, instead of buffering the table contents in memory. This is useful when we are dumping big tables, and we do not have enough memory to buffer the rows.

Options affecting the output

The following options affect the output of `mysqldump`: the contents of the dump itself.

The dump is not automatically written into a file. We have to redirect the output of `mysqldump`, or it will simply be displayed on our video. To redirect it, we can use the following syntax:

```
mysqldump ... > file_name
```

On Windows, an alternative is using the `--result-file=path` option. This is useful to produce files that can be safely read on any operating system.

- The `--character-set=str` option can be used to set the dump's character set. The default character set is UTF8.

- If the `--databases` and `--all-databases` options are specified, the resulting dump will include the CREATE DATABASE IF NOT EXISTS and CREATE TABLE IF NOT EXISTS statements by default. However, if we do not want to generate these statements, we can specify the `--no-create-db` and `--no-create-info` options.

- If the `--databases` and `--all-databases` options are not specified, no CREATE statement is generated. This is generally what we want, because it allows us to recreate the data into a database with a different name.

- If our dump contains the CREATE DATABASE and CREATE TABLE statements, we will probably want to delete those objects if they already exist. So we can use the `--add-drop-database` option, which adds the DROP DATABASE IF EXISTS statement, and `--add-drop-table`, which adds the DROP TABLE IF EXISTS statement.

- If we are not going to recreate the existing tables, we may want to decide how to deal with possible duplicates. We can specify the `--insert-ignore` option to generate `INSERT IGNORE` statements, or `--replace` to generate the `REPLACE` statements. If none of these clauses are used, the dump will contain normal `INSERT` statements.

- It is possible to group in a transaction all `INSERT` statements that refer to the same table. To do this, we can use the `--no-autocommit` option. It writes `SET autocommit = 0;` before each table, and `COMMIT;` after the insertions. Normally, this is not necessary to guarantee data integrity, and other connections trying to write into the table will have to wait until the end of the transaction. However, the insertion of data will be faster, because the write operations are grouped together.

- `--no-autocommit` is also useful for non-transactional tables, because it blocks concurrent `ALTER TABLE` operations. However, for these tables, the transaction will not block the other write operations. So, when dumping only or mostly the non-transactional tables, we may prefer to use `--add-locks` to add the `LOCK TABLES` and `UNLOCK TABLES` statements before and after each table data.

Usage examples for mysqldump

We discussed many `mysqldump` options. While each of them is quite easy to understand, there are a considerable number of options to remember, and some of them can easily be confused by a beginner. So, now it is time to show some examples.

To back up all the databases in our MariaDB installation, we can run:

```
mysqldump -uthurandot -psecret --all-databases --single-transaction >
eshop.sql
```

To back up our `eshop` database without the `CREATE` and `DROP` statements, we can give the following command:

```
mysqldump -uthurandot -psecret --single-transaction eshop > eshop.sql
```

To reload it, we will need to specify the default database:

```
mysql -uthurandot -psecret --database=eshop < eshop.sql
```

To back up our database with all the `CREATE` and `DROP` statements:

```
mysqldump -uthurandot -psecret –single-transaction --add-database-info
--add-drop-info --databases eshop > eshop.sql
```

To restore it, we will not need to specify a default database this time:

```
mysql -uthurandot -psecret < eshop.sql
```

To back up a single table:

```
mysqldump -uthurandot -psecret --single-transaction eshop product >
eshop.sql
```

Speeding up data import

When the data we need to load into the database is big, the import operation may be slow. Sometimes, however, there are some tricks that we can use to speed up things.

If the target tables have unique indexes or foreign keys, MariaDB verifies the consistency of the data we are loading. This operation is time-consuming. If we are sure that our data is correct, we may want to temporarily disable integrity checks for the current session. We can do this in the following way:

```
SET @@foreign_key_checks = OFF;
SET @@unique_checks = OFF;
```

Other connections will not be affected by this change. After loading the data, we can restore the integrity checks for the current session:

```
SET @@foreign_key_checks = ON;
SET @@unique_checks = ON;
```

If the target table is an InnoDB table, the lock used for guaranteeing unique AUTO_INCREMENT values can employ a strategy that is slightly less safe, but has better performance. We can do it in the following way:

```
SET @@global.innodb_autoinc_lock_mode = 2;
```

With InnoDB, the documentation also recommends turning off AUTOCOMMIT. If AUTOCOMMIT is enabled, the log will be flushed to the disk on every insert, and it will slow down the import. It can be disabled with the following command:

```
SET autocommit = 0;
```

Summary

In this chapter, we discussed two techniques to take database backups and restore them.

First we discussed how to generate a CSV file using `SELECT ... INTO OUTFILE`, and restore it with `LOAD DATA INFILE`. The flexibility provided by the `SELECT` statement can be a great advantage.

We also discussed the `mysqldump` tool that can be used to take a dump of our database. Then, we can run these files like any other file containing SQL statements.

In the final part, we learned some small tricks that can be used to speed up the loading of a backup.

In the next chapter, we will learn how to use *views* and *virtual columns* to have some data logic in your database instead of your application.

5
Views and Virtual Columns

Sometimes, we may want to shift some data logic from an application to the database. In order to do this, we can use two important features called views and virtual columns. These are objects that can be seen as tables or columns that are automatically populated with the data calculated by MariaDB. These features can also be used to add security to our database, or to solve some performance problems.

This chapter will cover the following topics:

- Views
- VIRTUAL columns
- PERSISTENT columns

Views

A **view** can be thought of as a virtual table. It is a query that has been saved in a database with a name. The rows returned by the saved query can be seen as table contents, and the set of columns that form the result set can be seen as the table structure. Most SQL statements can refer to a view as if it were a table, and the user who writes those queries may not even know that he/she is using a view.

In MariaDB, sometimes the tables are called **base tables** to highlight the fact that they are not views.

There can be several reasons for using a view. For example, views can:

- Avoid duplication of the same SQL code in several queries
- Minimize the impact of changes in the underlying tables on the SQL code
- Hide the complexity of the underlying tables
- Hide information from the underlying tables

We will explore these concepts later. First, let's see how views can be managed using SQL statements.

Views can be managed using the following statements:

- CREATE VIEW
- ALTER VIEW
- RENAME VIEW
- DROP VIEW

 Views, like tables, can be displayed with the SHOW TABLES command.

Creating or modifying a view

To create a view, we must use the CREATE VIEW statement, which has the following syntax:

```
CREATE [OR REPLACE]
    [ALGORITHM = {UNDEFINED | MERGE | TEMPTABLE}]
    [DEFINER = { user | CURRENT_USER }]
    [SQL SECURITY { DEFINER | INVOKER }]
    VIEW view_name [(column_list)]
    AS <select_query>
    [WITH [CASCADED | LOCAL] CHECK OPTION]
```

These clauses will be explained in the following subsections.

The ALTER VIEW statement is very similar to CREATE VIEW:

```
ALTER
    [ALGORITHM = {UNDEFINED | MERGE | TEMPTABLE}]
    [DEFINER = { user | CURRENT_USER }]
    [SQL SECURITY { DEFINER | INVOKER }]
    VIEW view_name [(column_list)]
    AS <select_query>
    [WITH [CASCADED | LOCAL] CHECK OPTION]
```

The only difference here is that there is no OR REPLACE clause, because it would make no sense to use it for this command.

So, to summarize, we have three ways of creating or altering a view:

- CREATE VIEW creates a view, or produces an error if the view exists
- ALTER VIEW modifies a view, or produces an error if the view does not exist
- CREATE OR REPLACE VIEW modifies the view if it exists, or creates the view if it does not exist

If we want to rename a view without changing its definition, we can use the RENAME statement, which we discussed in *Chapter 2, Databases and Tables*.

The SHOW TABLES statement, discussed in *Chapter 2, Databases and Tables*, also returns the existing views.

The SHOW CREATE TABLE statement can also be used on a view. There is a more specific SHOW CREATE VIEW statement as well, but it cannot be used on tables.

 Note that a view is always stored within a database, just like physical tables.

View limitations

While views can be thought of as logical tables, they are not written to disk. A view is merely a query with a name and some extra information used internally by MariaDB. When the optimizer receives a query that involves one or more views, it merges the views to the main query.

Because of the nature of views, two important limitations should be taken into account:

- Some queries cannot be used as a view
- Some views are not updatable

In the following subsections, we will learn more about these limitations.

Queries that cannot be used as a view

Queries used in view definitions are subject to the following limitations:

- Only SELECT queries can be used: SHOW commands, for example, are not allowed
- All referenced tables must exist at the time of creation of the view
- None of the tables referred in the SELECT query can be a temporary table
- Derived tables are not allowed
- Variables cannot be used

Note that, while all the referenced tables must exist at the time of creation of the view, they can be erased or replaced later. This feature makes views more flexible.

Updatable views

An **updatable view** is a view whose data can be modified directly. In other words, an updatable view can be used as a table in the INSERT, DELETE, UPDATE, and REPLACE statements. The data in non-updatable views can only be modified by changing the data in the underlying tables.

Let's see an example of an updatable view:

```
MariaDB [eshop]> CREATE OR REPLACE VIEW low_cost_product AS
    -> SELECT id, name, price, description
    -> FROM product
    -> WHERE price < 50;
Query OK, 0 rows affected (0.07 sec)
MariaDB [eshop]> SELECT id, name, price FROM low_cost_product;
+----+---------------+-------+
| id | name          | price |
+----+---------------+-------+
|  1 | Black T-Shirt | 25.00 |
|  2 | Red T-Shirt   | 25.00 |
+----+---------------+-------+
2 rows in set (0.00 sec)
MariaDB [eshop]> UPDATE low_cost_product SET price = 20.00 WHERE id = 2;
Query OK, 1 row affected (0.09 sec)
Rows matched: 1  Changed: 1  Warnings: 0
MariaDB [eshop]> SELECT id, name, price FROM low_cost_product;
```

```
+----+--------------+-------+
| id | name         | price |
+----+--------------+-------+
|  2 | Red T-Shirt  | 20.00 |
|  1 | Black T-Shirt| 25.00 |
+----+--------------+-------+
2 rows in set (0.00 sec)
MariaDB [eshop]> SELECT * FROM product;
+----+--------------+-------+----------+-------------+
| id | name         | price | quantity | description |
+----+--------------+-------+----------+-------------+
|  1 | Black T-Shirt| 25.00 |       25 | 0           |
|  2 | Red T-Shirt  | 20.00 |       25 | 0           |
+----+--------------+-------+----------+-------------+
2 rows in set (0.00 sec)
```

In the preceding example, we built a view called `low_cost_product` on the `product` table. It is an updatable view, so we were able to modify one row. The change is visible in both the view and the underlying table.

Now, let's see an example of a non-updatable view:

```
MariaDB [eshop]> CREATE OR REPLACE VIEW product_cost_stats AS
    -> SELECT AVG(price) price_avg, COUNT(*) product_count
    -> FROM product;
Query OK, 0 rows affected (0.06 sec)

MariaDB [eshop]> SELECT * FROM product_cost_stats;
+-----------+---------------+
| price_avg | product_count |
+-----------+---------------+
| 22.500000 |             2 |
+-----------+---------------+
1 row in set (0.01 sec)

MariaDB [eshop]> UPDATE product_cost_stats SET price_avg = 5.00;
ERROR 1288 (HY000): The target table product_cost_stats of the UPDATE is
not updatable
```

In the preceding example, we created a view called `product_cost_stats`, with the statistical data on the `product` table. Then we tried to update it, but we received an error that tells us that `product_cost_stats` is not an updatable view.

View security

Normally, a view references one or more underlying tables. The default behavior is that a user can read the data from the view only if he/she has the permissions to do so from the underlying tables.

View definers

This behavior can be changed by setting a definer for the view. A **definer** is usually the user who issues the CREATE VIEW statement, but the root user can arbitrarily set any other user as the definer. If a definer is set, MariaDB will check the definer's rights on the tables and columns referenced by the view.

To understand why this technique is useful, we will use an example. Suppose we have a table, `customer`, defined as follows:

```
CREATE TABLE customer (
    id INTEGER NOT NULL AUTO_INCREMENT PRIMARY KEY,
    first_name VARCHAR(50),
    last_name VARCHAR(50),
    birth_date DATE,
    sex ENUM('M', 'F'),
    email VARCHAR(255) NOT NULL,
    work_phone VARCHAR(30),
    cell_phone VARCHAR(30),
    newsletter TINYINT UNSIGNED NOT NULL
) ENGINE = InnoDB;
```

The table contains a lot of personal data about our customers, such as their name, their birth date, their sex, and different means to contact them (such as e-mail address, cell phone number, and so on). We have a newsletter that we use for informing our customers about our new services and promotions; customers subscribed to this newsletter have the `newsletter` field set to `1`.

The newsletter is sent via a PHP script. The developer who maintains this script has a MariaDB account to access the database. While this is probably necessary, suppose we want to restrict the information that he/she can access. The developer naturally needs to read the users' id, email, first_name, and last_name, but we want to prevent him/her from reading any other information, such as their phone numbers. Moreover, we would also like to prevent him/her from reading any information about the users who are not subscribed to the mailing list. We can achieve this via a view with a definer.

The first step is to create the view showing the information needed by the newsletter script:

```
CREATE DEFINER = CURRENT_USER SQL SECURITY DEFINER
  VIEW customer_mail AS
  SELECT id, first_name, last_name, email
    FROM customer
    WHERE newsletter = TRUE;
```

With this statement, we have created a view called customer_mail based on the customer table. If the current user has the permissions to query the customer table, the view will always work. Other users only need to have the SELECT privilege on the customer_mail view in order to run a table on it.

Now, suppose that the current user is root. We simply have too many permissions, and we don't want to assign them all to the view. Why? The reasons are not obvious, yet they are valid. For example, the root user can update and delete rows in any table, or insert new rows. To be sure that the underlying data will not be modified by the users who only have access to the view, we may want to set a definer different from root. Or the view could contain a bug which allows us to see too much data. Or again, we may want to delete the current user (perhaps it is someone other than root).

To explicitly set a definer, we can use this syntax:

```
CREATE DEFINER = bob SQL SECURITY DEFINER
  VIEW customer_mail AS
  SELECT id, first_name, last_name, email
    FROM customer
    WHERE newsletter = TRUE;
```

Now we have a view that only has access to data that can be seen by the user bob.

But let's get back to our newsletter example. Whichever definer we choose for the view, we have to create a user for the newsletter script who has the permissions necessary for reading the `customer_mail` view and nothing else. Let's see how:

```
CREATE USER 'newsletter' IDENTIFIED BY 'secret_word';

REVOKE ALL ON *.* FROM 'newsletter'@'%';

GRANT SELECT ON eshop.newsletter_mail TO 'newsletter'@'200.100.50.10';
```

The newsletter user will not have the rights to directly access the customer table or any other contents except the `customer_mail` view.

Constraints on inserts

Sometimes, updatable views have a WHERE clause. We have already created such a view:

```
CREATE OR REPLACE VIEW low_cost_product AS
  SELECT id, name, price, description
    FROM product
    WHERE price < 50;
```

Note that `low_cost_product` is an updatable view. While users who query this view can only read the low-cost products, they can insert products with any price. Moreover, they can change a product price, making it a high-cost product. More generally speaking, when an INSERT or UPDATE statement is issued, by default MariaDB does not check the WHERE clauses in a view.

The following example demonstrates this behavior:

```
MariaDB [test]> INSERT INTO product (name, price, description)
    -> VALUES ('laptop', 1200, '');
Query OK, 1 row affected (0.07 sec)
MariaDB [test]> SELECT * FROM low_cost_product WHERE price > 1000;
Empty set (0.00 sec)
MariaDB [test]> SELECT * FROM product WHERE price > 1000;
+----+--------+---------+----------+-------------+
| id | name   | price   | quantity | description |
+----+--------+---------+----------+-------------+
|  6 | laptop | 1200.00 |        0 |             |
+----+--------+---------+----------+-------------+
1 row in set (0.00 sec)
```

In the preceding example, we first inserted a record that didn't match the WHERE clause of `low_cost_product`. Then we queried `low_cost_product`, and verified that the record is not shown. However, when we queried the `product` table, the record was shown: it was definitely inserted.

While this is the default behavior, the CHECK OPTION clause can change it. If this clause is specified for a view, MariaDB will enforce the WHERE clause during the write operations as well. Insertions directed to a view will thus be blocked if the new record does not match the WHERE clause. Let's see an example:

```
MariaDB [test]> CREATE OR REPLACE VIEW low_cost_product AS
    -> SELECT id, name, price, description FROM product
    -> WHERE price < 50
    -> WITH CHECK OPTION;
Query OK, 0 rows affected (0.08 sec)
MariaDB [test]> INSERT INTO low_cost_product (name, price, description)
    -> VALUES ('laptop', 1200, '');
ERROR 1369 (HY000): CHECK OPTION failed 'test.low_cost_product'
```

The example shows that, if the CHECK OPTION is specified, insertions not matching the WHERE clause are rejected with an error.

In complex databases, a view could be built on another view. In this case, two variants of the CHECK OPTION clause can be used:

- WITH CASCADED CHECK OPTION: The underlying view's WHERE clauses will be enforced. This is the default behavior, used only if the WITH CHECK OPTION clause is specified.

- WITH LOCAL CHECK OPTION: Only the WHERE clause specified for the target view will be enforced. The WHERE clauses from the underlying views will be ignored.

Virtual and persistent columns

We described a view on a virtual table, meaning that its contents are the results of a query. The idea behind virtual columns is very similar: they are columns based on SQL expressions.

A virtual column overview

The terminology is a bit confusing here. In fact, all automatically calculated columns are called virtual columns in MariaDB KnowledgeBase. However, there are two types of virtual columns: VIRTUAL columns and PERSISTENT columns.

- A VIRTUAL column is calculated on-the-fly when it is referenced in a statement—for example, when a SELECT clause extracts its value. This is the default type.
- A PERSISTENT column is written in the table and its value can be read when needed, as happens with regular columns.

Calculating each value on-the-fly is additional work for the CPU, but saves space on the disk. Only PERSISTENT columns can be indexed or used in a foreign key.

In both cases, the calculated values cannot be directly inserted or modified. MariaDB automatically modifies these values when the columns involved in their calculations are modified.

Syntax for virtual columns

The syntax for creating a virtual column is the following:

```
<column_name> <column_type>   [GENERATED ALWAYS]   AS
(<sql_expression>) [VIRTUAL | PERSISTENT [UNIQUE] ]
[COMMENT <string>]
```

This syntax can be used in both the CREATE TABLE and the ALTER TABLE statements.

Note that there is no way to specify NULL or NOT NULL. However, if sql_expression never returns NULL, we could consider the column as a NOT NULL column.

The CHARACTER SET and COLLATION clauses are not supported either, but we can use the CONVERT() function to specify the desired character set. For example, the following expression always returns a utf8 string:

```
CONVERT(CONCAT(col_a, col_b) USING utf8)
```

Refer to the section on virtual column examples given later in this chapter for examples of the creation of VIRTUAL and PERSISTENT columns.

Limitations of virtual columns

Virtual columns have two important limitations: they can only be used with some storage engines, and the SQL expressions used for virtual columns are subject to some restrictions.

Storage engine support

Virtual columns need support at the storage engine level. Fortunately, most storage engines support them. The following storage engines are among those that support virtual columns:

- InnoDB
- MyISAM
- Aria
- CONNECT

If we try to create a table with a virtual column using a storage engine that does not support this feature, we will get an error. For example:

```
MariaDB [test]> CREATE TABLE t (
    -> num INT,
    -> square INT GENERATED ALWAYS AS (num * 2) VIRTUAL
    -> )
    -> ENGINE = MEMORY;
ERROR 1910 (HY000): MEMORY storage engine does not support computed
columns
```

Allowed expressions

The expressions used to calculate virtual values are subject to several limitations. The huge number of limitations should not discourage us: in fact, when there is a practical need for a virtual column, the column can be created. However, we should be aware of the types of expression that are allowed and those that are not.

These expressions:

- Must be based on at least one regular column.
- Cannot involve other virtual columns.
- Must not be constant.

- Must be deterministic: for each row, it must have one and only one possible value. Values such as random numbers, the current timestamp, or the current user cannot be involved in virtual columns' definitions.

- Cannot involve a subquery.

- Cannot involve a stored function or a user-defined function. These functions are not covered by this book; we will just state that this limitation exists for the sake of completeness.

There are also exceptions to the above rules:

- While the server's time zone can be configured at runtime, it is possible to use the CONVERT_TZ() function

- While the names of months and days are language-dependent, the DATE_FORMAT() and DAYNAME() functions are allowed

- Server variables, including dynamic variables, are allowed

- Expressions can involve or return FLOAT values, even though they may be considered as non-deterministic due to loss of precision

Compatibility with other database systems

Virtual columns are not a part of any standard SQL specification. However, many relational DBMSs support them with some differences and deficiencies.

MariaDB support for virtual columns was added in version 5.2. MySQL started supporting virtual columns after MariaDB, in version 5.7, with a slightly incompatible syntax.

> Currently, mysqldump does not enclose virtual columns' definitions in the executable comments. Therefore, restoring a dump of a database with virtual columns into a version of MariaDB or MySQL that does not support this feature requires some manual changes. Follow this bug to know when this limitation will be removed: https://mariadb.atlassian.net/browse/MDEV-5475.

Some of the DBMSs that support virtual columns are as follows:

- FirebirdSQL
- Oracle
- Microsoft SQL Server

In SQL Server, this feature is called *computed fields*.

Examples of virtual columns

Now, let's see some examples of virtual columns.

Taxed prices

The most common example is probably a virtual column containing a taxed price. So, let's get back to our `product` table. We will add a `tax` column, which represents the tax (`20` percent) applied to the `price` value.

```
ALTER TABLE product
  ADD COLUMN tax INTEGER AS ((price / 100) * 20) VIRTUAL;
```

We used a `VIRTUAL` column because calculating this value on-the-fly does not imply that much work for the CPU.

However, our applications usually show the taxed price to the users, and not just the tax amount. So, we will also add a `taxed_price` column:

```
ALTER TABLE product
  ADD COLUMN taxed_price INTEGER AS (price + (price / 100) * 20) VIRTUAL;
```

As mentioned earlier, a virtual column definition cannot contain a reference to another virtual column. Therefore, `(price + tax)` is not a legal expression; we have to repeat the percentage calculus here.

We defined two very similar columns, and we stated that one of them is rarely used. But a virtual column is not calculated unless a query contains an explicit reference to it, so we do not really care how often it is used.

One could object that the tax may depend on a certain number of factors, such as the state laws and the product type. Then, we may need to keep the information on taxes in a separate table. This can be true, but if this is the case we cannot use a virtual column. In fact, as explained previously, a virtual column definition cannot contain a subquery.

Indexing values

When a column is compared with the result of a function, no index can be used to speed up the comparison. For example, suppose we have the following table:

```
CREATE TABLE product_order
(
  id INTEGER UNSIGNED NOT NULL AUTO_INCREMENT PRIMARY KEY,
  date DATE NOT NULL,
```

```
    product_id INTEGER UNSIGNED NOT NULL,
    quantity SMALLINT UNSIGNED NOT NULL
)
    ENGINE = InnoDB;
```

 This table is not a good example of database design: it assumes that an order can include only one product type. But a simple design makes the examples clearer, so this table is good for our purposes.

At some point, say we want to know the average number of orders made in the current year, for each weekday. We can use the GROUP BY clause to do this:

```
SELECT WEEKDAY(date), COUNT(*)
    FROM product_order
    WHERE YEAR(date) = YEAR(NOW())
    GROUP BY WEEKDAY(date);
```

This query is correct, but no index will be used to solve the WHERE or the GROUP BY clause. This can make the query slow if the table is big. The reason is that indexes can be used to find a specific value of date, but not a specific value of YEAR(date).

To solve this problem, we can define two new PERSISTENT columns, and build two indexes on them:

```
ALTER TABLE product_order
    ADD COLUMN year SMALLINT UNSIGNED AS (YEAR(date)) PERSISTENT,
    ADD INDEX idx_year (year),
    ADD COLUMN weekdate TINYINT UNSIGNED AS (WEEKDAY(date)) PERSISTENT,
    ADD INDEX idx_weekday (weekdate);
```

Now, we can modify the query so that it uses the new indexed PERSISTENT columns:

```
SELECT weekday, COUNT(*)
    FROM product_order
    WHERE year = YEAR(NOW())
    GROUP BY weekday;
```

 PostgreSQL has a feature called **functional indexes**: it consists of indexing the result of a function. PostgreSQL users, who have switched to MariaDB and are searching for a replacement for functional indexes, can use indexed PERSISTENT columns.

Stricter UNIQUE constraints

The ideas shown in the previous example can be extended to build more expressive UNIQUE constraints.

For example, we could have a table containing documents sent by the users. The documents must have unique identifiers. However, if we use a normal UNIQUE index, the following identifiers are considered distinct:

- MariaDB howto
- MariaDB how to
- mariadb howto
- mariadb_howto

We want to avoid this. The uniqueness check should ignore the letters' case, spaces, and underscores. To do this, we need to convert the string to a case-insensitive collation, and remove the undesired characters. The result values can be stored in a PERSISTENT column with a UNIQUE index:

```
CREATE TABLE document
(
  id INTEGER UNSIGNED NOT NULL AUTO_INCREMENT PRIMARY KEY,
  name CHAR(20) NOT NULL,
  contents TEXT,
  normalized_name CHAR(20) AS (
    REPLACE(
      REPLACE(name COLLATE utf8_general_ci, '_', '')
      , ' ', ''
    )
  ) PERSISTENT UNIQUE
)
  ENGINE = InnoDB;
```

Summary

In this chapter, we discussed views and virtual columns. These topics are logically related, because views can be considered as virtual tables.

We examined views and learned how to manage or query them. We discussed their limitations, and some of the purposes for which they could be used. In particular, we learned how they can improve the database security.

Then we discussed virtual columns. This term includes both VIRTUAL and PERSISTENT columns; the former are calculated on-the-fly when needed, and the latter are stored on disk. We discussed how this feature can help us with some practical examples. The examples also showed how PERSISTENT columns can be used to build useful indexes, or to create powerful UNIQUE checks.

In the next chapter, we will talk about *dynamic columns* and understand the kind of problems they can solve.

6

Dynamic Columns

In this chapter, we will examine the problem of storing non-homogeneous data in the same table. The first part will discuss the approaches traditionally used in relational databases. The following part will examine a MariaDB feature which solves the problem in a totally different way: dynamic columns.

We will discuss the following topics in this chapter:

- The problem of storing non-homogeneous data
- Dynamic columns functions
- Nested dynamic columns
- Indexing dynamic columns

The problem: storing non-homogeneous data

In our database, we have a table called `product`. We defined it such that it only contains very generic attributes, like the product's `id`, `name`, `price`, the available `quantity`, and a `description`. But we will also need to store more specific attributes that depend on the product type: for example, for a shirt we will need to store the color and a size that is encoded as a character (S for small, M for medium, and so on); for a pair of shoes we will probably store the brand and the size, but in this case, the size is a number.

This is a typical problem we face every time we need to store heterogeneous data that could belong to the same logical class. Here, heterogeneous means that each entity has a variable number of specific attributes, and attributes with the same name could be of different types. How should we store heterogeneous data in a relational database?

There are several approaches to this problem. The optimal choice depends on the specific needs of a database and the applications that access it. In this section, we will discuss all the main approaches, and we will implement them in different databases: for example, the first approach will be implemented in the eshop_1 database. Eventually, in the next section, we will examine a MariaDB feature that can be used to solve the problem in a simple way: dynamic columns. Along with this explanation, we will see examples for implementing a solution with this feature in the eshop database. In the real world, we may find hybrid solutions, mixing multiple approaches together.

So, the approaches that we will discuss are:

- All data in the same table
- All data in separate tables
- Specific attributes in separate tables
- Relational representation of specific attributes
- Dynamic columns

Storing all product types in the same table

Storing heterogeneous data in the same table is generally the worst solution, but it can be viable if you only need to store two or three different object types with a very limited number of specific attributes.

This technique simply consists of creating a table containing all the attributes of the various product types. In our case, we could use the following table to store shirts and shoes:

```
CREATE OR REPLACE TABLE eshop_1.product
(
  id INTEGER UNSIGNED NOT NULL AUTO_INCREMENT PRIMARY KEY,
  name VARCHAR(50) NOT NULL,
  price DECIMAL(6, 2) NULL,
  quantity SMALLINT NOT NULL DEFAULT 0,
  description TEXT NOT NULL,
  product_type ENUM('shirt', 'show') NOT NULL,
  -- shirts attributes
  size_char VARCHAR(3),
  color VARCHAR(10),
  -- shoes attributes
```

```
  size_num TINYINT,
  brand VARCHAR(10)
)
  ENGINE = InnoDB
  CHARACTER SET = utf8
  COMMENT 'Catalogue of products on sale';
```

There is a `product_type` column that indicates if the attribute is a shirt or a pair of shoes. As the comments indicate, the `size_char` and `color` columns are used for shirts, while `size_num` and `brand` are used for shoes. All these specific columns can be set to NULL: for example, in rows that describe shirts, the `size_num` and `brand` columns will be NULL. Of course, this table could be a bit more relational; for example, we could have a separate table for brands, and another table for shirt colors. But we want to simplify our examples, as usual.

The only advantage of this model is that it tends to simplify the queries for a simple application. For example, if we want to know a product's average price, we will use a very simple query. And extracting the average price of the shirts is not any more complicated.

```
SELECT AVG(price) FROM eshop_1.product;
SELECT AVG(price) FROM eshop_1.product WHERE product_type = 'shirt';
```

However, note that for all product types, two columns are not significant. If we had more than two product types, the number of non-significant columns would grow, especially if a product type has many specific characteristics. For each column, we will need some space, and even more space will be wasted if some indexes are built on that column. Some indexes will be much less than optimal; for example, an index could be built on shirt-specific columns; but if most of the index entries are not related to shirts, operations on that index will not be as fast as they could be.

Maintaining the schema would also be difficult. Every time we need to add a product type, we will probably need to add more columns, and maybe some indexes. For big tables, these operations could be time consuming. Also, if we need to delete a product type, we will also need to drop its specific columns and indexes. But we will need to pay attention, because some of those columns could be used by other product types too.

 It should now be clear that we should never use this model.

Storing whole products in separate tables

Contrary to the previous approach, here the method consists of creating a table for each product type, and keeping the data for all the products in these tables. From a purely relational point of view, this is probably the cleanest approach.

In our example, we will not have a `product` table, but we will create the `shirt` and `shoe` tables:

```
CREATE OR REPLACE TABLE eshop_2.shirt
(
  id INTEGER UNSIGNED NOT NULL AUTO_INCREMENT PRIMARY KEY,
  name VARCHAR(50) NOT NULL,
  price DECIMAL(6, 2) NULL,
  quantity SMALLINT NOT NULL DEFAULT 0,
  description TEXT NOT NULL,
  size_char VARCHAR(3),
  color VARCHAR(10),
  INDEX idx_size (size_char)
)
  ENGINE = InnoDB
  CHARACTER SET = utf8
  COMMENT 'Catalogue of shirts on sale';

CREATE OR REPLACE TABLE eshop_2.shoe
(
  id INTEGER UNSIGNED NOT NULL AUTO_INCREMENT PRIMARY KEY,
  name VARCHAR(50) NOT NULL,
  price DECIMAL(6, 2) NULL,
  quantity SMALLINT NOT NULL DEFAULT 0,
  description TEXT NOT NULL,
  size_num TINYINT,
  brand VARCHAR(10),
  INDEX idx_size (size_num),
  INDEX idx_brand (brand)
)
  ENGINE = InnoDB
  CHARACTER SET = utf8
  COMMENT 'Catalogue of shoes on sale';
```

In the preceding example, the tables have some common fields as well as some specific fields. We also created some ad hoc indexes for each table. No space is wasted, because these columns and indexes are meaningful for each row.

Queries involving a particular product type are still very simple. For example, calculating the average price of the shirts is trivial:

```
SELECT AVG(price) FROM shirt;
```

However, queries involving multiple product types are less simple and less efficient, because a UNION is needed:

```
(SELECT AVG(price) FROM shirt)
UNION DISTINCT
(SELECT AVG(price) FROM shoe);
```

Maintenance is generally simpler with this mode: to add a product type, we will add a new table without modifying the existing ones; to drop a product type, we will simply drop a table. But things can be complicated when we need to add, drop, or modify a column that is used for all the product types: in this case, we will need to modify all the tables.

Storing product-specific attributes in separate tables

This is a hybrid approach. It consists of storing all the common attributes in a generic product table, while moving specific columns to separate tables.

The advantage of this solution is that you have all your products in the same table, and you need to make a JOIN only to read specific attributes.

In our case, it can be done as follows:

```
CREATE OR REPLACE TABLE eshop_3.product
(
  id INTEGER UNSIGNED NOT NULL AUTO_INCREMENT PRIMARY KEY,
  name VARCHAR(50) NOT NULL,
  price DECIMAL(6, 2) NULL,
  quantity SMALLINT NOT NULL DEFAULT 0,
  description TEXT NOT NULL,
  product_type ENUM('shirt', 'show') NOT NULL
)
```

```
  ENGINE = InnoDB
  CHARACTER SET = utf8
  COMMENT 'Catalogue of products on sale';
CREATE OR REPLACE TABLE eshop_3.shirt
(
  id INTEGER UNSIGNED NOT NULL AUTO_INCREMENT PRIMARY KEY,
  -- link to product table
  product_id INTEGER UNSIGNED NOT NULL,
  -- specific attributes
  size_char VARCHAR(3),
  color VARCHAR(10),

  FOREIGN KEY fk_shirt_product (product_id)
    REFERENCES product (id)
)
  ENGINE = InnoDB
  CHARACTER SET = utf8
  COMMENT 'Catalogue of products on sale';
```

The `product` table only contains the attributes that belong to all the product types. Then, we created a `shirt` table containing the shirt-specific attributes. There is also a link to the `product` table, with a foreign key that guarantees data integrity.

To insert a shirt into the database, we will do as follows:

```
INSERT INTO eshop_3.product SET
  name = 'Beatles T-shirt',
  price = 19.50,
  quantity = 200,
  description = 'A black T-shirt with Beatle\'s photos';
INSERT INTO eshop_3.shirt SET
  product_id = LAST_INSERT_ID(),
  size_char = 'XL',
  color = 'black';
```

With this technique, queries that only involve the common columns are easier and very fast. Other queries will generally require a JOIN. For example:

```
SELECT AVG(price) FROM product;
SELECT AVG(price)
  FROM shirt s
  LEFT JOIN product p
    ON s.product_id = p.id;
```

Between all the database patterns that we can use, this is the easiest to maintain: in no case will we need to repeat the same modification, or add the same index type on several tables.

Storing attributes in a relational table

This technique is the most flexible. It particularly suits situations when we do not know all the attributes that we will need to store in advance. The most obvious example is an application that is be used by several customers, each of them probably selling different types of products.

In this case, we will still have a product table, with columns that are meaningful for all the product types. But other product characteristics will be configured by the customer, so their definition will be stored in a separate table. Each attribute may be associated to one or more product types.

Finally, we will have a table containing the values for these attributes.

```
CREATE OR REPLACE TABLE eshop_4.product
  LIKE eshop_3.product;
CREATE OR REPLACE TABLE eshop_4.attribute_definition
(
  id INTEGER UNSIGNED NOT NULL AUTO_INCREMENT PRIMARY KEY,
  product INTEGER UNSIGNED NOT NULL,
  attribute_name CHAR(50) NOT NULL,
  attribute_description CHAR(255),
  FOREIGN KEY fk_attribute_product (product)
    REFERENCES product (id)
)
  ENGINE = InnoDB
  DEFAULT CHARACTER SET = utf8
  COMMENT 'Product characteristics definition';
```

```
CREATE OR REPLACE TABLE eshop_4.attribute_value
(
  attribute_id INTEGER UNSIGNED NOT NULL,
  attribute_value CHAR(255),
  FOREIGN KEY fk_attribute_value_definition (attribute_id)
    REFERENCES attribute_definition (id)
)
  ENGINE = InnoDB
  DEFAULT CHARACTER SET = utf8
  COMMENT 'Product characteristics definition';
```

In the preceding example, we used the CREATE TABLE ... LIKE statement to create a table with the same definition as the product table in the eshop_3 database.

Note that the attributes' definition and the attributes' values are stored in separate tables.

Again, this design is simplified to keep the examples easier to understand. In a real-world situation, to guarantee more flexibility, we would probably need a product_type table, and a many-to-many relation between product_type and attribute_definition. In this way, for each product, we would more clearly indicate its type; this would make integrity checks easier. Also, for each attribute definition, we may want to define some metadata like a minimum value, a maximum value, or other integrity rules.

Dynamic columns

Those who know languages similar to JavaScript can think of a dynamic column set as a dynamic object stored in the database in a binary format. Those who don't fully understand what a dynamic object is can think of dynamic column sets as column containers. At every moment it is possible to add or drop columns from these containers, as well as read them or get a list of columns. A dynamic column is a single attribute that can be created or manipulated in a set. This feature is a good way of storing non-homogeneous data in the same table.

 Dynamic columns were introduced in MariaDB 5.3, and were notably improved in MariaDB 10.0. This chapter only discusses the MariaDB 10.0 implementation.

Creating the dynamic columns container

A dynamic column needs to be stored in a binary column. This column can be of type TINYBLOB, BLOB, MEDIUMBLOB, or LONGBLOB. If the set can be empty, we will declare the column as NULL, because the NULL value is the only way to represent an empty dynamic columns set.

We will not create any index on the dynamic column set. If we need to index a particular attribute or a sequence of attributes, we will do this with a PERSISTENT column. The technique to do this is described later, in the *Indexing dynamic columns* section.

Now, let's get back to our example. We will create a dynamic columns set called characteristics, in our product table:

```
CREATE OR REPLACE TABLE product
(
    id INTEGER UNSIGNED NOT NULL AUTO_INCREMENT PRIMARY KEY,
    name VARCHAR(50) NOT NULL,
    price DECIMAL(6, 2) NULL,
    quantity SMALLINT NOT NULL DEFAULT 0,
    description TEXT NOT NULL,
    characteristics BLOB NOT NULL
)
    ENGINE = InnoDB
    CHARACTER SET = utf8
    COMMENT 'Catalogue of products on sale';
```

In the next section, we will see how we can manipulate the dynamic columns, and also look at examples for populating this BLOB column with data.

Dynamic column functions

In order to allow us to read and manipulate dynamic columns, MariaDB provides us with some specific functions. In this section, we will discuss these functions and some usage examples.

Creating dynamic columns

When a dynamic column set does not yet exist, a dynamic column can be created with COLUMN_CREATE(). The syntax is the following:

```
COLUMN_CREATE(<dyncol_name>, <dyncol_value> AS <type>)
```

When creating, modifying, or reading a dynamic column, we always need to specify its type. Only some types are allowed, and the size is optional.

> The complete list of the accepted data types can be found in the documentation at the following address: https://mariadb.com/kb/en/mariadb/dynamic-columns/#datatypes.

Parameters can be repeated a multiple number of times to add multiple columns.

This function is typically used when inserting a row. For example:

```
INSERT INTO product SET
    name = 'Another shirt'
  , price = 22.00
  , quantity = 50
  , description = 'A nice shirt'
  , characteristics = COLUMN_CREATE(
      'size', 'XL' AS CHAR
    , 'color', 'yellow' AS CHAR
  );
```

Obtaining a dynamic column set structure

It is possible to get the list of dynamic columns in a set using the COLUMN_GET() function; to check if a dynamic column exists, one can use the COLUMN_EXISTS() function. The syntaxes of these functions are as follows:

```
COLUMN_GET(<blob_column>)
COLUMN_EXISTS(<blob_column>, <column_name>)
```

Let's see these functions in action:

```
MariaDB [eshop]> SELECT
    ->    COLUMN_LIST(characteristics) AS dyncols
    -> , COLUMN_EXISTS(characteristics, 'size') AS size_exists
    -> FROM product \G
```

```
*************************** 1. row ***************************
    dyncols: `size`,`color`
size_exists: 1
1 row in set (0.00 sec)
```

Reading a dynamic column

To get a dynamic column value, we can use the COLUMN_GET() function:

```
COLUMN_GET(<blob_column>, <dyncol_name> AS <type>)
```

Let's use this function to get the value of our size column:

```
MariaDB [eshop]> SELECT
    -> COLUMN_GET(characteristics, 'size' AS CHAR) AS size
    -> FROM product
    -> WHERE id = LAST_INSERT_ID() \G
*************************** 1. row ***************************
size: XL
```

Adding a dynamic column

If a dynamic column set already exists, it is possible to add a dynamic column by using the COLUMN_ADD() function. Its syntax is the following:

```
COLUMN_ADD(<blob_column>, <dyncol_name>, <dyncol_value> AS <type>)
```

As with the COLUMN_CREATE() function, it is possible to repeat the dyncol_name and dyncol_value parameters a multiple number of times to add more than one column.

Let's see an example. We will add a dynamic column called shirt_type to the newly created row.

```
MariaDB [eshop]> UPDATE product
    -> SET characteristics = COLUMN_ADD(
    -> characteristics, 'shirt_type', 'polo' AS CHAR
    -> )
    -> WHERE id = LAST_INSERT_ID();
Query OK, 1 row affected (0.20 sec)
Rows matched: 1  Changed: 1  Warnings: 0
MariaDB [eshop]> SELECT COLUMN_LIST(characteristics) AS dyncols
    -> FROM product \G
```

```
*************************** 1. row ***************************
dyncols: `size`,`color`,`shirt_type`
1 row in set (0.00 sec)
```

Dropping a dynamic column

Similarly, it is possible to drop a dynamic column from a set using the
COLUMN_DELETE() function.

```
COLUMN_DELETE(<blob_column>, <dyncol_name>, <dyncol_value>)
```

Now, let's take a look at another example. Let's drop the shirt_type dynamic
column that we created with the last example:

```
MariaDB [eshop]> UPDATE product
    -> SET characteristics = COLUMN_DELETE(
    -> characteristics, 'shirt_type'
    -> )
    -> WHERE id = LAST_INSERT_ID();
Query OK, 1 row affected (0.11 sec)
Rows matched: 1  Changed: 1  Warnings: 0
MariaDB [eshop]> SELECT COLUMN_LIST(characteristics) AS dyncols
    -> FROM product \G
*************************** 1. row ***************************
dyncols: `size`,`color`
1 row in set (0.00 sec)
```

Converting a dynamic column set to JSON

It is possible to retrieve a whole dynamic column set as a JSON object. This can be
useful in situations where we want to pass this dynamic object to other applications.
The COLUMN_JSON() function can be used for this purpose; its syntax is the following:

```
COLUMN_JSON(<blob_column>)
```

For example, let's extract the shirt data from the previous examples as a JSON object:

```
MariaDB [eshop]> SELECT COLUMN_JSON(characteristics) AS shirt
    -> FROM product;
+--------------------------------+
| shirt                          |
+--------------------------------+
```

```
| {"size":"XL","color":"yellow"} |

+-------------------------------+

1 row in set (0.01 sec)
```

Checking the integrity of dynamic columns

If we always manipulate a dynamic column set using the functions explained in this section (COLUMN_CREATE(), and others), and we store it in a BLOB column, it should always contain valid data. User errors, such as manipulating the dynamic columns in other ways or storing them in TEXT columns can, however, corrupt the data. Moreover, we can never exclude the invalid values caused by factors like hardware failures, or even MariaDB bugs.

The COLUMN_CHECK() function checks if the passed dynamic column set is valid. If it is, the function returns 1, otherwise 0 is returned. Note that there is no function to repair a corrupted dynamic column set.

The COLUMN_CHECK() syntax is as follows:

```
COLUMN_CHECK(<blob_column>)
```

```
SELECT COLUMN_CHECK(characteristics) FROM product;

+-------------------------------+
| COLUMN_CHECK(characteristics) |
+-------------------------------+
|                             1 |
+-------------------------------+

1 row in set (0.00 sec)
```

Nesting dynamic columns

Using the COLUMN_CREATE() function, we can also create nested dynamic columns. Doing this is quite simple: we will use the COLUMN_CREATE() function itself to generate a dynamic column value. Consider the following example:

```
SET @box = COLUMN_CREATE(
    'white box', 'pen'
  , 'brown box', COLUMN_CREATE(
      'green box', 'pencil'
    , 'blue box', 'paper'
  )
);
```

We have two outer boxes: the white box and the brown box. The white box contains a pen. The brown box contains two more boxes (the green and blue boxes), so its content is the value returned by another COLUMN_CREATE() invocation.

Now, let's see how to read the nested values:

```
MariaDB [eshop]> SELECT COLUMN_GET(
    -> COLUMN_GET(@box, 'brown box' AS CHAR)
    -> , 'green box' AS CHAR
    -> ) AS green_box \G
*************************** 1. row ***************************
green_box: pencil
1 row in set (0.00 sec)
```

Let's look at the preceding query. With the outer COLUMN_GET() invocation, we want to extract the content of the green box. But we cannot directly extract that value from the @box variable, because the 'green box' attribute is nested. So the dynamic column set for the green box is the result of another COLUMN_GET() that extracts the value of 'brown box'.

However, if we are using nested dynamic columns, we are unlikely to know their structure in advance. Thus, we will probably want to get the whole set as a JSON object, as follows:

```
MariaDB [eshop]> SELECT COLUMN_JSON(@box) AS boxes;
+-----------------------------------------------------------------------+
| boxes                                                                 |
+-----------------------------------------------------------------------+
| {"brown box":{"blue box":"paper","green box":"pencil"},"white
box":"pen"} |
+-----------------------------------------------------------------------+
1 row in set (0.00 sec)
```

Note that while the COLUMN_JSON() function is recursive, it reads a maximum of 10 nested levels. However, having such a complex structure stored in the MariaDB dynamic columns may not be a good idea, because the performance will probably be too poor.

Storing multiple dynamic column containers in the same table

Suppose that a table contains dynamic columns that can logically be divided into two or more groups. For each column, we can tell *a priori* which group it belongs to. Moreover, we will often need to read or modify only one of these groups. In this case, we will want to store the groups in different BLOB columns. This could make our queries more readable, and probably faster.

Indexing dynamic columns

An index cannot be directly built on a dynamic column. This can reduce the performance of the dynamic columns, especially when used as a filter, or for sorting the results. However, it is possible to define a virtual column of the PERSISTENT type on a dynamic column, and build an index on it.

In the next example, we will build an index on the size attribute:

```
ALTER TABLE product
  ADD COLUMN size CHAR(3) AS (COLUMN_GET(characteristics, 'size' AS
CHAR(3))) PERSISTENT,
  ADD INDEX idx_size (size);
```

To create a PERSISTENT column with the size attribute, we used an expression based on COLUMN_GET(). Here, we specified a column size (3 characters), because we want the indexes to be as small as possible.

Building a virtual column on a dynamic column that is only set for some rows, and indexing this column, may look like a waste of memory. However, this is largely balanced by the performance gain derived from the use of an index.

Summary

In this chapter, we started by examining the possible techniques used to represent heterogeneous data in a relational database. All the approaches we discussed have some pros and some cons, so the best choice depends on our needs.

Then, we discussed dynamic columns. They solve the problem in an easy way, by treating a table column as a dynamic object. In fact, different rows can have different dynamic columns. Attributes can even be added or dropped at any time. We examined the functions used to do this. We also demonstrated that dynamic columns can be nested.

In the last section, we built a PERSISTENT virtual column on a dynamic column, and then indexed the PERSISTENT column. This is a very important technique, because it is the only way to index a dynamic column.

In the next chapter, you will learn how to make full-text search queries with MariaDB.

7
Full-Text Searches

You are now able to build the next generation e-commerce platform but your search engine is not really efficient. You might like to search for multiple words in the name and description fields of your products, make complex queries, exclude words, or retrieve documents containing several specified words.

In order to achieve that, you will have to add the full-text search functionality to your database. Full-text searches give you the same power as any decent search engine. Moreover, a relevance score is given to each result so that you can sort the results that you show to your customers.

In this chapter, we will cover the following topics:

- Defining full-text search
- Full-text searches in MySQL and MariaDB
- Working with full-text indexes
- Full-text queries
- Mroonga
- Connecting MariaDB to Sphinx

Defining a full-text search

Instead of performing a search against the metadata or a part of the original text represented in a database, a full-text search examines all the words of all the documents stored in the database, and tries to match the search criteria.

A full-text search is able to identify natural-language documents that satisfy a query, and optionally to sort them by relevance to the query. This is often used to retrieve all the documents containing a list of terms.

For a large number of documents, it's not possible to examine all documents for every single query. Thus, we create indexes for specific terms that we might probably use as criteria in our future queries. With these indexes, it's faster to find the documents in which the specified terms are used.

With standard text searches, it's not possible to use indexes in most of the SQL databases, and for every query, the database engine has to scan the whole table. That's why full-text searches are useful, even if it's only to find the documents containing just one term.

Full-text searches also include a notion of relevance or ranking. Depending on the frequency of a term in the documents, the size of the documents and other such factors, the documents matching the criteria get a relevance score.

Full-text searches also introduce the possibility of making flexible searches with Boolean operators to exclude documents containing certain words, or to give a higher score to some words.

Full-text searches in MySQL and MariaDB

Until MySQL 5.6, full-text searches were only available with the MyISAM tables. But since full-text searches were implemented in InnoDB, you can also use them with this engine.

As for MySQL, MariaDB provides full-text searches with the MyISAM tables and with the Aria tables, which are the crash-safe alternative to MyISAM. Full-text searches have also been implemented in InnoDB with MariaDB 10.0.5. But the real difference from MySQL has been the introduction of a new storage engine, Mroonga, in MariaDB 10.0.15. This storage engine allows the use of a full-text search engine, Groonga, via SQL.

Working with full-text indexes

In order to perform full-text searches on a table, you must index the data. In MariaDB, the type of index used for full-text searches is named FULLTEXT.

A full-text index can only be created on a column of type CHAR, VARCHAR, or TEXT.

As with the other indexes, the FULLTEXT index can be created by using CREATE TABLE when creating a new table, or by using ALTER TABLE or CREATE INDEX on an already existing table.

The following code will create a table, `posts`, with a full-text index on the `content` column:

```
CREATE TABLE `posts` (
  `id` int(11) NOT NULL AUTO_INCREMENT,
  `title` varchar(255) NOT NULL,
  `content` text,
  PRIMARY KEY (`id`),
  FULLTEXT (`content`)
) ENGINE=InnoDB;
```

If you already have a table without a full-text index, there are two ways of adding a full-text index to a column. One way is by using ALTER TABLE:

```
ALTER TABLE `posts` ADD FULLTEXT(`content`);
```

The other way is by using CREATE INDEX:

```
CREATE FULLTEXT INDEX `content` ON `posts` (`content`);
```

If you want to remove an index, you must use the following query:

```
ALTER TABLE `posts` DROP INDEX `content`;
```

Please note that the indexes are updated every time you add new data to your table. If you want to import a large dataset into your table, it would be faster to first remove the index, then import the data, and finally re-create the index.

Full-text queries

There are three different modes of full-text queries. The default mode, which is the natural language mode, will only search documents containing at least one of the words that you have specified. The Boolean mode allows you to make more complex queries by using different operators to exclude words, to give a higher relevance to certain words, or to search for a specific phrase instead of unlinked words. The last mode, called *query expansion search*, will first perform a natural language search in order to retrieve the most relevant terms from the resulting rows. Those terms will then be added to the query, which will be executed again.

In the following section, we will use the *Sakila Sample Database*. Please install it by following the instructions given on the MySQL website at http://dev.mysql.com/doc/sakila/en/sakila-installation.html.

The natural language mode

In this mode, MariaDB will look for rows that are relevant to the specified query using natural human language. It's close to the way humans phrase a search query, and provides results ranked the same way they would be if you were using a search engine—for example, "How to make a full-text search with MariaDB?".

For each query, a relevance score will be computed and represented by a positive floating-point number. If there are no matches, the relevance will be zero. Various factors are used to calculate the relevance, such as the number of words in the record, the total number of words in the table, the number of records matching the search criteria, or the number of repetitions of the words of the query in a record.

The natural language search is done with the MATCH() and AGAINST() functions. The column where you want to search is specified with the MATCH() function, and the search expression is specified with the AGAINST() function.

Using the Sakila sample database, we can extract all the documentaries from the list of films that we have by searching for the word *documentary* in the description. The query will be as follows:

```
SELECT * FROM film_text WHERE MATCH(title,description)
AGAINST('documentary');
```

You would obtain a list of 101 films. Observe that the rows are not sorted by the primary key, but by another criteria. Earlier, we had discussed the fact that a relevance score is assigned to each row of the result. MariaDB returns the search results in descending order of relevance.

If you use the following query, you can display the relevance score:

```
SELECT film_id, MATCH(title,description) AGAINST('documentary')
as relevance FROM film_text WHERE MATCH(title,description)
AGAINST('documentary');
```

Now if you want to watch a documentary about space, you may try the following query:

```
SELECT * FROM film_text WHERE MATCH(title,description)
AGAINST('documentary space');
```

As you can see in the results, you now have 145 matching films, while earlier you had only 101 documentaries. When performing a query in the natural language mode, MariaDB will try to find at least one of the words in the query. That's why you get all the documentaries and all the films about space.

You can use the following query to verify the relevance:

```
SELECT MATCH(title,description) AGAINST('documentary space') as
relevance, description FROM film_text WHERE MATCH(title,description)
AGAINST('documentary space');
```

The first results will be as follows:

```
+-------------------+---------------------------------------------------------
--------------------------------------------------------------------------------
--------+
| relevance         | description
|
+-------------------+---------------------------------------------------------
--------------------------------------------------------------------------------
--------+
|   4.592566967010498 | A Fanciful Documentary of a Womanizer And
a Boat who must Defeat a Madman in The First Manned Space Station
|
|   4.546156883239746 | A Awe-Inspiring Documentary of a Woman And a
Husband who must Sink a Database Administrator in The First Manned Space
Station        |
|   4.546156883239746 | A Beautiful Documentary of a Boat And a Sumo
Wrestler who must Succumb a Database Administrator in The First Manned
Space Station  |
|   4.339165687561035 | A Fateful Documentary of a Crocodile And a
Husband who must Face a Husband in The First Manned Space Station
|
|   2.707171678543091 | A Emotional Reflection of a Teacher And
a Man who must Meet a Cat in The First Manned Space Station
|
|   2.707171678543091 | A Astounding Panorama of a Man And a
Monkey who must Discover a Man in The First Manned Space Station
|
|   2.707171678543091 | A Astounding Saga of a Dog And a Boy
who must Kill a Teacher in The First Manned Space Station
|
```

You can see that only the results with the highest relevance (four in this case) contain all the words that you used in your query, and will give you relevant results. All the other rows contain only one of the words, and are not documentaries about space.

By using more words and taking only the most relevant results, you can find results which are closer to what you expect. Another example is the following query:

```
SELECT MATCH(title,description) AGAINST('documentary space database')
as relevance, description FROM film_text WHERE MATCH(title,description)
AGAINST('space documentary database');
```

However, there is another way to get exactly what you asked for, without having to add new words or care about the relevance score.

The Boolean mode

This mode allows you to use special operators to improve your query.

To use the Boolean mode, you need to add the IN BOOLEAN MODE modifier to your query.

The following operators are available:

Operator	Description
+	The word is mandatory in all the rows returned.
-	The word cannot appear in any of the rows that are returned.
<	The word that follows has a lower relevance than other words, although the rows containing it will still match.
>	The word that follows has a higher relevance than other words.
( )	Used to group words into subexpressions.
~	The word following this contributes negatively to the relevance of the row (which is different to the '-' operator, which specifically excludes the word, or the '<' operator, which still causes the word to contribute positively to the relevance of the row).
*	The wildcard, indicating zero or more characters. It can only appear at the end of a word.
"	Anything enclosed in the double quotes is taken as a whole (so you can match phrases, for example).

For your documentary about space, you will use the following query:

```
SELECT * FROM film_text WHERE MATCH(title,description)
AGAINST('+documentary +space' IN BOOLEAN MODE);
```

It will return the only four documentaries about space. You can notice that they are ordered by the primary key, and no longer by the relevance score.

Now, if you want to search for a film about a sumo wrestler that is not a documentary, you can use the following query:

```
SELECT * FROM film_text WHERE MATCH(title,description) AGAINST('+sumo
-documentary' IN BOOLEAN MODE);
```

Query expansion

The last type of full-text search is done using query expansion. In certain situations, you may want to search for information using implicit knowledge. For example, if you search for MySQL or MariaDB, it will likely be related to databases. To widen the result of the search, MariaDB will add new words to the query to find more results. It's very useful when you enter only a few short keywords to return more results.

MariaDB will first execute the query using the language query mode. Then it will extract all the relevant words from the results, and perform a final query by using the previous words and the new words.

You will need to add the WITH QUERY EXPANSION modifier to be able to use the query expansion mode.

We will create a new table with new data to test this feature. Create the table, and add the data with the following query:

```
CREATE TABLE ft2(copy TEXT, FULLTEXT(copy)) ENGINE=MyISAM;
INSERT INTO ft2(copy) VALUES
  ('MySQL vs MariaDB database'),
  ('Oracle vs MariaDB database'),
  ('PostgreSQL vs MariaDB database'),
  ('MariaDB overview'),
  ('Foreign keys'),
  ('Primary keys'),
  ('Indexes'),
  ('Transactions'),
  ('Triggers');
```

We will first run a standard query using the natural language mode:

```
SELECT * FROM ft2 WHERE MATCH(copy) AGAINST('database');
```

The results contain all the records containing the word `database` as expected:

```
+------------------------------+
| copy                         |
+------------------------------+
| MySQL vs MariaDB database    |
| Oracle vs MariaDB database   |
| PostgreSQL vs MariaDB database |
+------------------------------+
```

Now we will run the following query using query expansion:

```
SELECT * FROM ft2 WHERE MATCH(copy) AGAINST('database' WITH QUERY
EXPANSION);
```

Since the word MariaDB is often found next to the word database, it has been added to the query, and you get the following result:

```
+------------------------------+
| copy                         |
+------------------------------+
| MySQL vs MariaDB database    |
| Oracle vs MariaDB database   |
| PostgreSQL vs MariaDB database |
| MariaDB overview             |
+------------------------------+
```

If you try the query expansion modifier on the Sakila database, you will notice that you will obtain all the rows of the table for almost every search. The query expansion modifier returns a lot of non-relevant results, and increases noise significantly. You should use it only when the keyword is short, or if you don't return enough results in the default mode.

Limitations to the full-text search

The full-text search done with MyISAM, Aria, and InnoDB has some limitations.

- Short words with less than four characters are ignored, and are not stored in the full-text index.

- Long words with more than 84 characters are also ignored and absent from the full-text index.

- There is a list of stopwords which are common words and are ignored. These words differ depending on the storage engine. It doesn't apply to the Boolean mode.

- The words which appear in more than half of the rows are considered irrelevant and are excluded from the results, except if you are using the Boolean mode.

 The list of stopwords can be found in the MariaDB knowledge base at `https://mariadb.com/kb/en/mariadb/stopwords/`.

Mroonga

If you try to perform full-text searches in a document in the Chinese, Japanese, or Korean languages, you will notice that it either doesn't work very well or not at all.

The default full-text search feature uses spaces to separate words in a document. However, these languages usually do not use spaces as delimiters. As a result, standard full-text search engines are ineffective with the CJK languages. Moreover, these languages contain many words with less than four characters. So, the standard search method is not adapted at all, as it ignores short words with four or less characters by default.

A project was started in 2008 to try and solve this problem. The project was called Senna, and it tried to add Japanese language support to the full-text search feature of MySQL.

From 2011 onwards, a new project called Groonga, presented as the successor of Senna, started providing regular releases of a generic library that provides connections to different DBMSs. Mroonga is the MySQL storage engine that interfaces with Groonga.

To sum up, if you need to do full-text searches in the Chinese, Japanese, or Korean languages, you will need Mroonga to do the job. Mroonga provides CJK-ready full-text searches, and is faster than the MyISAM and InnoDB full-text searches for both updating and searching.

Installation

Mroonga is not enabled by default. You will need to run the following command in your MariaDB console to enable it:

```
INSTALL SONAME 'ha_mroonga';
```

You can now check that it's correctly loaded by running the following:

```
SHOW ENGINES;
```

One last thing that you can do to make it work is to add a user-defined function:

```
CREATE FUNCTION last_insert_grn_id RETURNS INTEGER SONAME 'ha_mroonga.
so';
```

This function is provided by Mroonga, but you need to register it to be able to use it later. It allows you to return the record ID that was assigned by the last INSERT.

Mroonga modes

Mroonga can work in two different modes:

- In the first mode, the storage mode, Groonga is used for both the full-text search function and the data storage.
- In the second mode, the wrapper mode, data are still stored in another storage engine like InnoDB, but Groonga is used for the full-text search related operations while other operations are done by the existing storage engine. This mode allows InnoDB to be used as a storage engine, and Mroonga for providing a fast full-text search engine.

Creating a table

You will now learn how to create a table using the storage mode and the wrapper mode.

The storage mode

To use the storage mode, you need to specify ENGINE = Mroonga when creating your table.

Let's try to create a table with some data:

```
CREATE TABLE diaries (
    id INT PRIMARY KEY AUTO_INCREMENT,
    content VARCHAR(255),
```

```
    FULLTEXT INDEX (content)
) ENGINE = Mroonga DEFAULT CHARSET utf8;
```

```
INSERT INTO diaries (content) VALUES ("It'll be fine tomorrow."), ("It'll
rain tomorrow");
```

The wrapper mode

To use the wrapper mode, you need to add an SQL comment like COMMENT =
'engine "InnoDB"' to specify the storage engine.

Your query for creating the table will now be as follows:

```
CREATE TABLE diaries (
    id INT PRIMARY KEY AUTO_INCREMENT,
    content VARCHAR(255),
    FULLTEXT INDEX (content)
) ENGINE = Mroonga COMMENT = 'engine "InnoDB"' DEFAULT CHARSET utf8;
```

Full-text queries

Now, we can try a full-text search:

```
SELECT * FROM diaries WHERE MATCH(content) AGAINST("fine");
```

You should get the following result from the preceding search:

```
+----+-------------------------+
| id | content                 |
+----+-------------------------+
|  1 | It'll be fine tomorrow. |
+----+-------------------------+
1 row in set (0.00 sec)
```

The basic full-text search is working as expected.

We will now try to get the relevance score. Add the following data to your table:

```
INSERT INTO diaries (content) VALUES ("It's fine today. It'll be fine
tomorrow as well."), ("It's fine today. But it'll rain tomorrow.");
```

We now have more data, and can try the following query:

```
SELECT *, MATCH (content) AGAINST ("fine") as relevance FROM diaries
WHERE MATCH (content) AGAINST ("fine") ORDER BY relevance DESC;
```

You should obtain the following result:

```
+----+--------------------------------------------------+-----------+
| id | content                                          | relevance |
+----+--------------------------------------------------+-----------+
|  3 | It's fine today. It'll be fine tomorrow as well. |    233018 |
|  1 | It'll be fine tomorrow.                          |    116509 |
|  4 | It's fine today. But it'll rain tomorrow.        |    116509 |
+----+--------------------------------------------------+-----------+
```

Note that the results are not sorted by the relevance score by default, and you have to order them yourself.

Choosing a different parser

Several parsers are available for full-text search in Mroonga.

For example, with the default parser no results will be returned if you run the following search:

```
SELECT * FROM diaries WHERE MATCH(content) AGAINST("day");
```

However, if you change the parser with the following queries, two results will be returned:

```
ALTER TABLE `diaries` DROP INDEX `content`;

ALTER TABLE `diaries` ADD FULLTEXT(`content`) COMMENT 'parser
"TokenBigramSplitSymbolAlpha"';
```

In the storage mode, the parser is selected by using an SQL comment. You can select the parser when adding an index, as we have done in the last example. Otherwise, you can specify it when creating your table:

```
CREATE TABLE diaries (
    id INT PRIMARY KEY AUTO_INCREMENT,
    content VARCHAR(255),
    FULLTEXT INDEX (content) COMMENT 'parser
"TokenBigramSplitSymbolAlpha"'
) ENGINE = Mroonga DEFAULT CHARSET utf8;
```

The available parsers are the following:

Parser	Description
`off`	No tokenizing is performed.
`TokenBigram`	Default value. It tokenizes in bigram, but continuous alphabetical characters, numbers, or symbols are treated as a token. It's possible to have tokens with three or more letters to reduce the noise.
`TokenBigramIgnoreBlank`	Same as `TokenBigram` except that white spaces are ignored.
`TokenBigramIgnoreBlankSplitSymbol`	Same as `TokenBigramSplitSymbol` except that white spaces are ignored.
`TokenBigramIgnoreBlankSplitSymbolAlpha`	Same as `TokenBigramSplitSymbolAlpha` except that white spaces are ignored.
`TokenBigramIgnoreBlankSplitSymbolAlphaDigit`	Same as `TokenBigramSplitSymbolAlphaDigit` except that white spaces are ignored.
`TokenBigramSplitSymbol`	Same as `TokenBigram` except that continuous symbols are not treated as a token, but tokenized in bigram.
`TokenBigramSplitSymbolAlpha`	Same as `TokenBigram` except that continuous alphabetical characters are not treated as a token, but tokenized in bigram.
`TokenDelimit`	Tokenizes by splitting on white spaces.
`TokenDelimitNull`	Tokenizes by splitting on null characters (\0).
`TokenMecab`	Tokenizes using MeCab. Requires Groonga to be built with MeCab support.
`TokenTrigram`	Tokenizes in trigrams, but continuous alphabetical characters, numbers, or symbols are treated as a token.
`TokenUnigram`	Tokenizes in unigrams, but continuous alphabetical characters, numbers, or symbols are treated as a token.

The Boolean mode

Mroonga also supports the Boolean mode to do the searches. However, there are fewer operators, as you can see in the following list:

Qualifier	Description
+	A leading plus sign indicates that this word must be present in each row that is returned.
–	A leading minus sign indicates that this word must not be present in any of the rows that are returned.
*	The asterisk serves as the truncation (or wildcard) operator.
"	A phrase that is enclosed within the double quote characters matches only the rows that contain the phrase literally, as it was typed.
()	Parentheses group words into subexpressions.

We will try the Boolean mode with the data added by the following queries:

```
CREATE TABLE books (
    `id` INTEGER AUTO_INCREMENT,
    `title` text,
    PRIMARY KEY(`id`),
    FULLTEXT INDEX title_index (title)
) ENGINE=mroonga default charset utf8;
INSERT INTO books (title) VALUES ('MariaDB'), ('MariaDB Groonga'),
('MariaDB Groonga Mroonga');
```

The following query will return all the records, and will compute a score depending on the number of words from the query present in the records:

```
SELECT title, MATCH (title) AGAINST('Groonga Mroonga' IN BOOLEAN MODE) AS
score FROM books;
```

You should obtain the following result:

```
+-------------------------+-------+
| title                   | score |
+-------------------------+-------+
| MariaDB                 |     0 |
| MariaDB Groonga         |     1 |
| MariaDB Groonga Mroonga |     2 |
+-------------------------+-------+
```

With the + operator, only the records with all the specified words will have their score computed.

```
SELECT title, MATCH (title) AGAINST('+Groonga +Mroonga' IN BOOLEAN MODE)
AS score FROM books;
```

You can also embed a pragma at the beginning of the query to specify how to execute it. For example, with the + operator, the query will become as follows:

```
SELECT title, MATCH (title) AGAINST('*D+ Groonga Mroonga' IN BOOLEAN
MODE) AS score FROM books;
```

For both of the two previous queries, you should obtain the same result:

```
+-------------------------+-------+
| title                   | score |
+-------------------------+-------+
| MariaDB                 |     0 |
| MariaDB Groonga         |     0 |
| MariaDB Groonga Mroonga |     2 |
+-------------------------+-------+
```

 Please consult the Mroonga documentation for more examples of the usage of Boolean operators in the Boolean mode. `http://mroonga.org/docs/reference/full_text_search/boolean_mode.html`.

Connecting MariaDB to Sphinx

Mroonga is a new full-text search engine, and the main goal is to support the CJK languages. Until now, the most-used search engine is probably Sphinx, which has a lot of features, allows you to perform very complex queries, and performs better than the other full-text search engines.

Sphinx is a full-text search engine designed to provide better performance and relevance than the standard full-text search features shipped by default with a variety of DBMSs. Sphinx can be integrated directly with the SQL databases, or be queried directly from a script.

There are three different ways to use Sphinx. The first way is to use SphinxQL, a small SQL subset. The second is the native search API, SphinxAPI. And the last, which we will use in this chapter, is a MySQL pluggable storage engine, SphinxSE.

The key features of Sphinx are:

- High indexing and searching performance
- Advanced indexing and querying tools
- Advanced result set post-processing
- Proven scalability up to billions of documents, terabytes of data, and thousands of queries per second
- Easy scaling with distributed searches

Installation

As with Mroonga, the Sphinx storage engine (SphinxSE) is also not enabled by default. Use the following query to enable it:

```
INSTALL SONAME 'ha_sphinx';
```

 Until MariaDB 10.0, SphinxSE was statically compiled into the MariaDB server for the Debian and Ubuntu packages, and the previous step was not required.

You can confirm that it is enabled with the following query:

```
SHOW ENGINES;
```

You will also need to install Sphinx on your server, because SphinxSE doesn't actually store any data and is only a client to the Sphinx daemon, which manages all the indexing and searching. You can find the instructions for installing Sphinx in the MariaDB documentation at https://mariadb.com/kb/en/mariadb/installing-sphinx/.

Configuration

Before being able to use Sphinx with MariaDB, you will need to configure some settings. The default configuration file to edit is called sphinx.conf. Depending on your OS, you will find it at /etc/sphinxsearch, /etc/sphinx or C:\Sphinx.

We will use the sample configuration file provided with Sphinx as well as the sample data. After editing the MariaDB connection information, you should obtain the following:

```
source src1
{
        type                    = mysql

        sql_host                = 127.0.0.1
        sql_user                = root
        sql_pass                = root
        sql_db                  = test
        sql_port                = 3306 # optional, default is 3306

        sql_query               = \
            SELECT id, group_id, UNIX_TIMESTAMP(date_added) AS date_
added, title, content \
            FROM documents

        sql_attr_uint           = group_id
        sql_attr_timestamp      = date_added

        sql_query_info          = SELECT * FROM documents WHERE id=$id
}


index test1
{
        source                  = src1
        path                    = /var/data/test1
        docinfo                 = extern
        charset_type            = sbcs
}


index testrt
{
```

```
        type                    = rt
        rt_mem_limit            = 32M


        path                    = /var/data/testrt
        charset_type            = utf-8


        rt_field                = title
        rt_field                = content
        rt_attr_uint            = gid
}



indexer
{
        mem_limit               = 32M
}

searchd
{
        listen                  = 9312
        listen                  = 9306:mysql41
        log                     = /var/log/searchd.log
        query_log               = /var/log/query.log
        read_timeout            = 5
        max_children            = 30
        pid_file                = /var/log/searchd.pid
        max_matches             = 1000
        seamless_rotate         = 1
        preopen_indexes         = 1
        unlink_old              = 1
        workers                 = threads # for RT to work
        binlog_path             = /var/data
}
```

The `sql_query` setting contains the query used by Sphinx for building the index.

The `sql_host`, `sql_user`, `sql_pass`, `sql_db`, and `sql_port` variables should be used to specify the connection details to your MariaDB database, which you defined earlier when you installed MariaDB.

We will now create the corresponding test database in MariaDB with the following queries:

```
DROP TABLE IF EXISTS test.documents;
CREATE TABLE test.documents
(
    id        INTEGER PRIMARY KEY NOT NULL AUTO_INCREMENT,
    group_id  INTEGER NOT NULL,
    group_id2  INTEGER NOT NULL,
    date_added  DATETIME NOT NULL,
    title      VARCHAR(255) NOT NULL,
    content    TEXT NOT NULL
);


REPLACE INTO test.documents ( id, group_id, group_id2, date_added, title,
content ) VALUES
    ( 1, 1, 5, NOW(), 'test one', 'this is my test document number one.
also checking search within phrases.' ),
    ( 2, 1, 6, NOW(), 'test two', 'this is my test document number two' ),
    ( 3, 2, 7, NOW(), 'another doc', 'this is another group' ),
    ( 4, 2, 8, NOW(), 'doc number four', 'this is to test groups' );


DROP TABLE IF EXISTS test.tags;
CREATE TABLE test.tags
(
    docid INTEGER NOT NULL,
    tagid INTEGER NOT NULL,
    UNIQUE(docid,tagid)
);


INSERT INTO test.tags VALUES
    (1,1), (1,3), (1,5), (1,7),
    (2,6), (2,4), (2,2),
    (3,15),
    (4,7), (4,40);
```

For the settings to take effect, restart Sphinx with the proper restart command depending on your operating system: `service sphinxsearch restart` for Debian and Ubuntu, or `service searchd restart` for Red hat and CentOS, or `systemctl restart sphinxsearch` or `systemctl restart searchd` respectively for operating systems using `systemd`.

The last step before being able to use Sphinx is to create a table, which will be used to add the search queries to be forwarded to Sphinx. You won't directly add data into this table; you will only read this table, and Sphinx will return the results of your queries through this table.

You can create a table with the following query:

```
CREATE TABLE t1
(
    id          BIGINT UNSIGNED NOT NULL,
    weight      INTEGER NOT NULL,
    query       VARCHAR(3072) NOT NULL,
    group_id    INTEGER,
    INDEX(query)
) ENGINE=SPHINX CONNECTION="sphinx://localhost:9312/test1";
```

The structure of this special table must follow a few rules:

- The first column will contain the document ID of the records returned by the query. The type of this field must be `BIGINT`.

- The second column will contain the relevance score, also called *match weight*, and must be an `INTEGER` or a `BIGINT`.

- The third column will contain your query, and must be a `VARCHAR` or a `TEXT` field.

- The following fields will be mapped from the source table using (`text.documents` in this particular case) the column names.

- The column names of the first three columns (`id`, `weight`, and `query` in the `t1` table) are ignored by Sphinx, as their structure is fixed.

Usage

Now that we have Sphinx running with a test database, we can start using it.

With Sphinx, both query text and search options should be located in the `WHERE` clause of the search `query` column. The query text and the search options are separated by semicolons.

If we want to search the records containing the word `document`, we would use the following query:

```
SELECT d.* FROM t1 LEFT JOIN documents as d ON t1.id = d.id WHERE
t1.query='document';
```

Since SphinxSE returns the primary key of the records which satisfy the query, we have to make a join to get the actual records.

If you want to get the records which contain several words, you can use the extended syntax.

```
SELECT d.* FROM t1 LEFT JOIN documents as d ON t1.id = d.id WHERE
t1.query='document & phrases;mode=extended';
```

The `extended` mode is enabled by using the mode `option`. The `&` operator is the logical AND.

You can also use the extended syntax to search for a phrase:

```
SELECT d.* FROM t1 LEFT JOIN documents as d ON t1.id = d.id WHERE
t1.query='"test document";mode=extended';
```

You can also use the field search operator to search only in one column.

```
SELECT d.* FROM t1 LEFT JOIN documents as d ON t1.id = d.id WHERE
t1.query='@title test;mode=extended';
```

Among the options provided by Sphinx, there are the `sort`, `offset`, and `limit` options, which replace the ORDER BY and LIMIT SQL clauses. It's faster to rely on these options and not use the SQL clauses.

> For an overview of all the available options, please consult the MariaDB documentation at `https://mariadb.com/kb/en/mariadb/about-sphinxse/`.
>
> Sphinx is a powerful full-text search engine with features beyond the scope of this book. Please consult the Sphinx documentation to learn how to make complex queries at `http://sphinxsearch.com/docs/archives/1.10/searching.html`.

Summary

You now understand what is meant by full-text searches and the reason why you need them. You now know how to use full-text searches with the standard storage engine of MariaDB. You also know how to use the Mroonga engine to make faster queries and support the CJK languages. You are also able to set up Sphinx and SphinxSE as powerful full-text engines behind your SQL database.

In the next chapter, you will learn to use the CONNECT storage engine with MariaDB. Unlike everything we have seen until now, this storage engine will allow us to access data stored in different formats in external files.

8
Using the CONNECT Storage Engine

If you are working in the Business Intelligence domain, or have to do some Business Intelligence tasks, you may find most of the tasks tedious. The CONNECT engine is here to solve this problem, and allows you to connect external data sources to MariaDB. You will also be able to make some data transformations directly with the CONNECT engine, without having to write complex queries.

This chapter will also tell you more about the community, its members and its goal, and where to find help or more information now that you have acquired a lot of knowledge about MariaDB.

In this chapter, we will cover the following topics:

- Understanding the CONNECT storage engine
- Accessing CSV files
- Accessing XML and HTML files
- The XCOL table type
- The OCCUR table type
- The PIVOT table type
- MariaDB community
- MariaDB resources
- Included storage engines

Understanding the CONNECT storage engine

The CONNECT storage engine has been designed for accessing data from external sources using MariaDB. This engine is not designed for OLTP, that is, you should not use it as the main engine for storing the data in your application. In fact, the data are never stored in MariaDB. The CONNECT storage engine should be used for Business Intelligence tasks such as creating data from the different sources available in one place.

Usually, the BI tasks are done through an ETL, then the data are computed, and specific tools are used for the reporting. Thanks to the CONNECT storage engine, standard tables can be used to access external data from MariaDB.

In other words, the CONNECT storage engine allows you to query external data by using the SQL language.

On some distributions, the library for the engine is not packaged directly with MariaDB. For example, for Debian and Ubuntu, you need to install the `mariadb-connect-engine-10.0` package.

To enable the CONNECT storage engine, you need to run the following command in your MariaDB console:

```
INSTALL SONAME 'ha_connect';
```

In this book, we will learn how to use only a few of the table types that are available. If you want to have more information about the available and supported data sources, please consult the documentation at `https://mariadb.com/kb/en/mariadb/connect-table-types-overview/`.

Accessing CSV files

The CSV file format is probably one of the most used formats for exchanging data between different applications that don't use the same format by default. Most of the spreadsheet software and RDBMSs have a function for importing and exporting data to the CSV format.

For BI, it can be used to centralize the data written by non-IT people with their favorite spreadsheet editor, such as employee lists, expense reports, sales reports, marketing statistics, and so on.

For example, if your bank lets you export your account activity in CSV, the format of the export will probably be similar to the following:

```
Date;Description;Debit;Credit;Balance
2015/08/01;"ATM Withdrawal";200.00;;7818.35
2015/07/27;"ATM Withdrawal";200.00;;8018.35
2015/07/26;"Bank transfer";1000.00;;8218.35
2015/07/25;"Bank transfer";;4000.00;9218.35
2015/07/20;"ATM Withdrawal";200.00;;5218.3
```

By default, the CONNECT storage engine will look for files in the MariaDB data directory, which is set to `/var/lib/mysql` by default. It's also possible to specify the absolute path. For this chapter, we will create a new `/tmp/mariadb` directory to store our files. After creating the aforementioned directory, create a new `/tmp/mariadb/bank.csv` file with the preceding CSV data.

We can now create the SQL table for accessing the data with the following query:

```
CREATE TABLE bank_account (
    `date` DATE NOT NULL date_format='YYYY/MM/DD',
    `description` VARCHAR(255) NOT NULL,
    `debit` FLOAT(12,2) UNSIGNED,
    `credit` FLOAT(12,2) UNSIGNED,
    `balance`  FLOAT(12,2)
) engine=CONNECT table_type=CSV
file_name='/tmp/mariadb/bank.csv'
header=1
sep_char=';'
quoted=1;
```

The structure of the table is exactly the same as the CSV file. We indicate to MariaDB to use the CONNECT engine, and that the source data is a CSV file. The `file_name` option allows us to specify the full path or the name of the file. As our CSV file includes column names in the first row, we use the `header` option to make the CONNECT engine skip the first row of the CSV file, and only insert data from the second row. The `sep_char` option lets you specify the column delimiter.

For the `quoted` option, the following values are possible:

- 0, to write between the quotes only the values which contain the column delimiter.
- 1, to quote only the text fields. The NULL fields do not get quoted.
- 2, to quote all the fields, except for the NULL fields.
- 3, to quote all the fields, including NULL fields.

You can now read your CSV file directly from MariaDB with the following query:

```
SELECT * FROM bank_account;
```

You can also insert data into the CSV file with the following query:

```
INSERT INTO bank_account VALUES('2015-08-02', 'Restaurant', 15, NULL,
7813.35);
```

If you check your file, a new line has been inserted at the end:

```
2015/08/02;"Restaurant";15.00;0.00;7813.35
```

> To be able to write data in a file, MariaDB must have write access to it. This can be done by using the chmod command, or by changing the owner of the file. For this example and the following ones, we will change the owner of the directory and the files present in it: `chown -R mysql /tmp/mariadb/`.

If you want to create a table with a column order different from that of the CSV files, you need to use the `flag` option:

```
DROP TABLE bank_account;
CREATE TABLE bank_account (
  `date` DATE NOT NULL date_format='YYYY/MM/DD',
  `description` VARCHAR(255) NOT NULL,
  `credit` FLOAT(12,2) UNSIGNED flag=4,
  `debit` FLOAT(12,2) UNSIGNED flag=3,
  `balance` FLOAT(12,2)
) engine=CONNECT table_type=CSV
file_name='/tmp/mariadb/bank.csv'
header=1
sep_char=';'
quoted=1;
```

Accessing XML and HTML files

XML is another widely used format for exchanging data between various softwares. The document can be represented by a tree, and each node can have one or several attributes.

In this chapter, we will use a sample file taken from the MSXML documentation at `https://msdn.microsoft.com/en-us/library/ms762271(v=vs.85).aspx`. Save this file in the previously created `/tmp/mariadb` folder as `books.xml`.

Accessing XML data

We will now create a table called `books` to access the XML data from MariaDB:

```
CREATE TABLE books (
  author VARCHAR(255),
  title VARCHAR(100),
  genre VARCHAR(100),
  price FLOAT(12,2),
  publish_date DATE date_format='YYYY-MM-DD',
  description VARCHAR(4096)
)
engine=CONNECT table_type=XML file_name='/tmp/mariadb/books.xml';
```

The column names of the table are mapped to the tags of the XML files. You can check that the mapping is done correctly, and that you can access your data with the following query:

```
SELECT * FROM books;
```

In the original file, there is an `id` attribute on the `book` tag, but it's not present in our table. To access the ID attribute, we need to use the `field_format` option:

```
DROP TABLE books;
CREATE TABLE books (
  id VARCHAR(5) field_format='@',
  author VARCHAR(255),
  title VARCHAR(100),
  genre VARCHAR(100),
  price FLOAT(12,2),
  publish_date DATE date_format='YYYY-MM-DD',
```

```
    description VARCHAR(4096)
)

engine=CONNECT table_type=XML file_name='/tmp/mariadb/books.xml';
```

The @ sign indicates that the value should not be taken from a child of the node, but from the attributes of the tag.

As for the CSV tables, you can also insert data into an XML file if the right permissions have been set on the file.

We will now try the case where your XML file contains more complex data, for example a tree with a height above one. We will create a new table to manipulate the data in a new file based on the previous example, but where the structure has slightly changed, as in the following example:

```
<book id="bk101">
    <author>
        <last>Gambardella</last>
        <first>Matthew</first>
    </author>
    <title>XML Developer's Guide</title>
    <genre>Computer</genre>
    <price>44.95</price>
    <publish_date>2000-10-01</publish_date>
    <description>An in-depth look at creating applications
    with XML.</description>
</book>
```

Create a /tmp/mariadb/books2.xml file following this structure.

```
CREATE TABLE books2 (
  id VARCHAR(5) field_format='@',
  author_firstname VARCHAR(255) field_format='author/first',
  author_lastname VARCHAR(255) field_format='author/last',
  title VARCHAR(100),
  genre VARCHAR(100),
  price FLOAT(12,2),
  publish_date DATE date_format='YYYY-MM-DD',
  description VARCHAR(4096)
)

engine=CONNECT table_type=XML file_name='/tmp/mariadb/books2.xml';
```

Here we used the `field_format` option to select the child of a child of the node, but it can be used to go deeper into the tree, or just to use the column names that don't match the tag names.

Detecting the data structure

MariaDB can also detect the data structure for you, and choose the columns to create in your table. This happens automatically if you don't specify a structure. Try the following query:

```
CREATE TABLE books2_auto engine=CONNECT table_type=XML file_name='/tmp/mariadb/books2.xml';
```

We can now view the generated columns with the following query:

```
SHOW CREATE TABLE books2_auto;
```

A result similar to the following should be returned:

```
CREATE TABLE `books2_auto` (
  `id` char(5) NOT NULL `FIELD_FORMAT`='@',
  `author` char(20) NOT NULL,
  `title` char(38) NOT NULL,
  `genre` char(15) NOT NULL,
  `price` char(5) NOT NULL,
  `publish_date` char(10) NOT NULL,
  `description` char(162) NOT NULL
) ENGINE=CONNECT `TABLE_TYPE`='XML' `FILE_NAME`='/tmp/mariadb/books2.xml';
```

We can see that it generates a column for each attribute and tag of the first level. But, for example, the children of the `author` tag have been concatenated together.

> More options are available to help you handle more complex XML files. Please consult the official documentation at the following address for more information: `https://mariadb.com/kb/en/mariadb/connect-xml-table-type/`.

Working with HTML data

The CONNECT engine doesn't directly support HTML, but if your HTML is formatted following the XML standard (xHTML), MariaDB will be able to read it.

We will create a new HTML file to export our bank account data, which was previously imported from a CSV file. To achieve that, we will first create an empty table, `bank_account_html`, which will create a new empty HTML file, and the data will be inserted with the following queries:

```
CREATE TABLE bank_account_html (
   `date` DATE NOT NULL date_format='YYYY/MM/DD',
   `description` VARCHAR(255) NOT NULL,
   `debit` FLOAT(12,2) UNSIGNED NOT NULL,
   `credit` FLOAT(12,2) UNSIGNED NOT NULL,
   `balance`  FLOAT(12,2) NOT NULL
) engine=CONNECT table_type=XML file_name='/tmp/mariadb/bank.html'
tabname='table' option_list='rownode=tr,colnode=td';
INSERT INTO bank_account_html SELECT * FROM bank_account;
```

Now, if you check the content of the `/tmp/mariadb/bank.html` file, you can see an HTML table:

```
<?xml version="1.0" encoding="UTF-8"?>
<!-- Created by the MariaDB CONNECT Storage Engine-->
<table>
        <tr>
                <td><date>2015/08/01</date></td>
                <td><description>ATM Withdrawal</description></td>
                <td><debit>0.00</debit></td>
                <td><credit>200.00</credit></td>
                <td><balance>0.00</balance></td>
        </tr>
        <tr>
                <td><date>2015/07/27</date></td>
                <td><description>ATM Withdrawal</description></td>
                <td><debit>0.00</debit></td>
                <td><credit>200.00</credit></td>
                <td><balance>0.00</balance></td>
        </tr>
        <tr>
                <td><date>2015/07/26</date></td>
                <td><description>Bank transfer</description></td>
                <td><debit>0.00</debit></td>
```

```
              <td><credit>1000.00</credit></td>
              <td><balance>0.00</balance></td>
        </tr>
        ...
</table>
```

The `tabname` option has been used to specify the root node name. The `rownode` option specifies the name of the first level node containing the data, while the `colnode` option is used to enclose the tags containing the values by another special tag.

Using the XCOL table type

The XCOL table is used when you have a table with a field containing a list of elements, and you want to access all these elements individually.

First, let's create a table with some data using the following queries:

```
CREATE TABLE anime (
   title VARCHAR(50) NOT NULL,
   characters VARCHAR(250) DEFAULT NULL
) ENGINE=CONNECT;
INSERT INTO anime VALUES
('Fullmetal Alchemist', 'Edward Elric, Alphonse Elric, Roy Mustang, Maes
Hughes, Greed, Riza Hawkeye, Alex Louis Armstrong'),
('Steins;Gate', 'Rintarou Okabe, Kurisu Makise, Mayuri Shiina, Itaru
Hashida'),
('Clannad: After Story', 'Tomoya Okazaki, Nagisa Furukawa, Ushio
Okazaki');
```

The first column contains the title of a Japanese anime, and the second column contains the names of the main characters.

 If you want to use a source table which doesn't use the CONNECT engine, you will need to provide more options. Please consult the documentation at https://mariadb.com/kb/en/mariadb/connect-table-types-proxy-table-type/.

Now, if we want to create a table with one row per character, we can create an XCOL table with the following query:

```
CREATE TABLE xanime ENGINE=CONNECT TABLE_TYPE=XCOL TABNAME=anime OPTION_
LIST='colname=characters';
```

The `TABNAME` option specifies the table that the XCOL table should use as source data. The `COLNAME` option is used to specify the column that should be split.

You can now display the data with the following query:

```
SELECT * FROM xanime;
```

It is worth noting that, as for the other CONNECT engine's table, the data are not copied and the data stays in the source table.

Now, let's compare the results of the following two queries:

```
SELECT COUNT(*) FROM xanime;
```

```
SELECT COUNT(characters) FROM xanime;
```

The first query returns 3, but the second returns 14. In fact, when you make a query which doesn't involve the column you want to split, the split is not done, and the source table is used as it is.

For the same reason, if you want to count the characters in each anime, you must specify the special column in the `count` function. The query will be the following:

```
SELECT title, COUNT(characters) FROM xanime GROUP BY title;
```

If you want to give a rank to each character present in each anime, the `ROWNUM` special column is useful.

```
CREATE TABLE xanime2 (
   rank int NOT NULL SPECIAL=ROWNUM,
   title VARCHAR(50) NOT NULL,
   characters VARCHAR(50) NOT NULL flag=2
)
ENGINE=CONNECT TABLE_TYPE=XCOL TABNAME=anime OPTION_
LIST='colname=characters';
```

If you want to display only the first main character of each anime, you can use the following query:

```
SELECT * FROM xanime2 WHERE rank = 1;
```

Using the OCCUR table type

The OCCUR table type allows you to create a new view of a table. A new row will be created for each cell of the table, the row will contain the name of the row, the name of the column, and the value in the corresponding cell.

We will first create a standard table with some data for practice:

```
CREATE TABLE `visitors` (
   `year` char(4) NOT NULL,
   `Jan` int(10) NOT NULL DEFAULT '0',
   `Feb` int(10) NOT NULL DEFAULT '0',
   `Mar` int(10) NOT NULL DEFAULT '0',
   `Apr` int(10) NOT NULL DEFAULT '0',
   `May` int(10) NOT NULL DEFAULT '0',
   `Jun` int(10) NOT NULL DEFAULT '0',
   `Jul` int(10) NOT NULL DEFAULT '0',
   `Aug` int(10) NOT NULL DEFAULT '0',
   `Sep` int(10) NOT NULL DEFAULT '0',
   `Oct` int(10) NOT NULL DEFAULT '0',
   `Nov` int(10) NOT NULL DEFAULT '0',
   `Dec` int(10) NOT NULL DEFAULT '0'
) ENGINE=CONNECT;
INSERT INTO visitors VALUES
('2015', 121, 172, 199, 181, 108, 199, 171, 156, 170, 183, 105, 176),
('2014', 167, 108, 137, 161, 198, 104, 129, 132, 172, 167, 119, 196),
('2013', 120, 116, 117, 140, 148, 119, 154, 112, 101, 166, 131, 156),
('2012', 189, 175, 112, 132, 127, 141, 121, 186, 165, 169, 148, 136),
('2011', 134, 162, 108, 158, 163, 144, 129, 116, 193, 117, 105, 176);
```

Each row of this table contains visitor statistics for one year, and each column represents a month.

To obtain one row for each year/month, we will create a new OCCUR table with the following query:

```
CREATE TABLE xvisitors (
   year char(4) NOT NULL,
   month char(3) NOT NULL,
   number int(10) NOT NULL
```

```
) ENGINE=CONNECT TABLE_TYPE=OCCUR
TABNAME=visitors
OPTION_LIST='OccurCol=number,RankCol=month'
Colist='Jan,Feb,Mar,Apr,May,Jun,Jul,Aug,Sep,Oct,Nov,Dec';
```

The TABNAME option specifies the source table. The OccurCol option specifies the column in which you will read the value of the cells extracted from your table. The RankCol option specifies the column in which you will read the column name coming from the source table. The Colist is the list of columns containing the cells with the date which will be put in the column specified by the OccurCol option.

You can display the resulting data with the following query:

```
SELECT * FROM xvisitors;
```

 As for the XCOL table, if the query doesn't contain the occurrence column, the data will not be mapped.

You should obtain a result similar to the following:

```
+------+-------+--------+
| year | month | number |
+------+-------+--------+
| 2015 | Jan   |    121 |
| 2015 | Feb   |    172 |
| 2015 | Mar   |    199 |
| 2015 | Apr   |    181 |
| 2015 | May   |    108 |
| 2015 | Jun   |    199 |
| 2015 | Jul   |    171 |
....
| 2011 | Aug   |    116 |
| 2011 | Sep   |    193 |
| 2011 | Oct   |    117 |
| 2011 | Nov   |    105 |
| 2011 | Dec   |    176 |
+------+-------+--------+
```

Every cell of the source table now has its own row, with the year and the month in the two first columns.

Using the PIVOT table type

The PIVOT table type allows you to do exactly the reverse operation of the OCCUR table. Let's start by creating a copy of our data in a new table.

```
CREATE TABLE xvisitors2 (
  year char(4) NOT NULL,
  month char(3) NOT NULL,
  number int(10) NOT NULL
) ENGINE=CONNECT;
INSERT INTO xvisitors2 SELECT * FROM xvisitors;
```

Now we can create a new PIVOT table:

```
CREATE TABLE pvisitors ENGINE=CONNECT TABLE_TYPE=PIVOT
TABNAME=xvisitors2;
```

You should now be used to the `TABLE_TYPE` and `TABNAME` options, which specify the table type and the source table respectively.

 If you have issues when creating this table, and get an `Access denied` error, please consult the documentation about proxy on non-CONNECT tables at https://mariadb.com/kb/en/mariadb/connect-table-types-proxy-table-type/.

You can now run the following query to check if the PIVOT operation has been realized:

```
SELECT * FROM pvisitors;
```

Since we didn't specify any option when creating the table, MariaDB considered the last column of the source table as the facts column, and then it took the last remaining column as the pivot column. MariaDB then constructed the new table from this information.

Now let's try to add some data with the following query:

```
INSERT INTO xvisitors2 VALUES ('2016', 'Jan', 15), ('2016', 'Jan', 42);
```

If you execute the previous `SELECT` query, you will see that both the rows have been summed up. That's the default behavior, but it can be changed using the `Function` option.

For example, if we want to calculate the average of the rows, we can achieve this result by using the following query:

```
CREATE TABLE pvisitors2 ENGINE=CONNECT TABLE_TYPE=PIVOT
TABNAME=xvisitors2

OPTION_LIST='PivotCol=month,Function=AVG';
```

Here, we have added the `PivotCol` option which is not required, but can be useful if you don't want to use the second to last column of the source table.

The MariaDB community

MariaDB has been created by Michael "Monty" Widenius, the founder of MySQL, Monty Program Ab (which is now the MariaDB Corporation), and a founding member of the MariaDB Foundation, with the aim of being a backward compatible drop-in replacement for MySQL.

The goal of the MariaDB Foundation is to ensure that there is not just one entity that drives the development of MariaDB, and that the official MariaDB development tools stay open to the MariaDB developer community.

The core team is not only composed of members of the MariaDB Foundation, but of outsiders as well. Most companies and people working on MariaDB have joined the Foundation. This is the case because participating or committing code is not a prerequisite for being a part of the Foundation.

MariaDB resources

We have covered a lot of topics in this book, but not everything. Here is a list of useful resources for finding more information on the topics discussed in this book, to discover other features, or to get help from the MariaDB experts.

The MariaDB website (`https://mariadb.org`) is the first place you should search. You can find the download links for MariaDB, the MariaDB blog, and other official MariaDB information at this website.

The second source of information is the MariaDB Knowledge Base (`https://mariadb.com/kb/en/`). The complete documentation, the release notes, and change logs can be found in the Knowledge Base. The documentation is often updated and you will always find information about the most recent features.

If you want to get in touch with other MariaDB users, there are several ways to do so.

You can use the IRC channel, where you can start a real-time chat with other people. As indicated in the Knowledge Base (`https://mariadb.com/kb/en/meta/irc/`), the official channel is `#maria` on the Freenode IRC network.

If you want to reach out to more people, you should probably use one of the following mailing lists:

- The MariaDB discuss list (`https://launchpad.net/~maria-discuss`) for general discussions about MariaDB.
- The MariaDB docs list (`https://launchpad.net/~maria-docs`) for discussions about the documentation and the Knowledge Base.
- The MariaDB developers list (`https://launchpad.net/~maria-developers`) for MariaDB developers or to follow the development of MariaDB.

You can also submit issues on the MariaDB JIRA (`https://mariadb.org/jira`). The JIRA is used for project planning, and for following MariaDB development.

Finally, you can also find MariaDB on the major social media platforms:

- Twitter (`https://twitter.com/mariadb`)
- Google+ (`https://plus.google.com/+mariadb`)
- Facebook (`https://www.facebook.com/MariaDB.dbms`)

Included storage engines

In addition to the storage engines present in MySQL, MariaDB also includes the following storage engines:

- Aria, which is a crash-safe alternative to the MyISAM engine
- XtraDB, which is a drop-in replacement for the InnoDB engine
- FederatedX, which is a drop-in replacement for the Federated engine
- OQGRAPH, which is used to store complex graphs and tree structures
- SphinxSE, which is used for full-text searches
- TokuDB, which provides increased compression and better performance, particularly adapted to write-intensive environments
- Cassandra, which allows access to data that are in a Cassandra cluster from MariaDB
- CONNECT, which allows access to external data in different formats

- SEQUENCE, which is used to generate sequences of numbers
- Spider, which allows the set up of clustering and sharding between several MariaDB servers

Summary

In this chapter, you learned what the CONNECT engine is, and the purpose it should be used for. You also learned how to read and write CSV, XML, and HTML data directly from MariaDB. Then we went deeper into the CONNECT engine, and used the XCOL, OCCUR, and PIVOT tables to transform data.

In the end, you also learned more about the MariaDB community, and some general information about the third-party plugins and storage engines distributed with MariaDB.

To sum up, in this book you first learned how to pick the right version of MariaDB for your needs, how to install MariaDB on the different operating systems, and how to use the console client. After that, we reviewed together the basics of relational databases, and the SQL language implementation used by MariaDB. Then we talked more about the advanced features such as data import and export, views, and virtual columns and dynamic columns. Finally, we discussed the advanced features of MariaDB that are not present in MySQL, full-text searches, and the CONNECT storage engine.

Index

T

table definition 32
tables
  creating 31
  displaying 32
  joining 75
  temporary tables, creating 33
table subqueries 80-82
table types
  reference link 164
temporal types 37, 38
times and dates
  extracting 91
  temporal values, writing 90
  time intervals, adding 90
  time intervals, subtracting 90
  working with 89
transaction
  about 57-59
  autocommit mode 59
  limitations 60, 61

U

unions 79
UNIX timestamp 38
updatable view
  about 112
  example 112-114

V

views
  about 109, 110
  constraints, on inserts 116, 117
  creating 110, 111
  definers 114-116
  limitations 111
  modifying 110, 111
  queries, limitations 112
  security 114
  updatable view 112-114

virtual columns
  about 117
  database system compatibility 120
  limitations 119
  limitations, with expressions 119, 120
  overview 118
  PERSISTENT column 118
  storage engine support 119
  syntax 118
  VIRTUAL column 118
virtual columns, examples
  indexing values 121, 122
  stricter UNIQUE constraints 123
  taxed prices 121

W

Windows
  MariaDB, installing 3

X

XCOL table type
  using 171, 172
XML files
  accessing 167
  data structure, detecting 169
  XML data, accessing 167-169
XOR operator 87, 88

Thank you for buying
MariaDB Essentials

About Packt Publishing

Packt, pronounced 'packed', published its first book, *Mastering phpMyAdmin for Effective MySQL Management*, in April 2004, and subsequently continued to specialize in publishing highly focused books on specific technologies and solutions.

Our books and publications share the experiences of your fellow IT professionals in adapting and customizing today's systems, applications, and frameworks. Our solution-based books give you the knowledge and power to customize the software and technologies you're using to get the job done. Packt books are more specific and less general than the IT books you have seen in the past. Our unique business model allows us to bring you more focused information, giving you more of what you need to know, and less of what you don't.

Packt is a modern yet unique publishing company that focuses on producing quality, cutting-edge books for communities of developers, administrators, and newbies alike. For more information, please visit our website at www.packtpub.com.

About Packt Open Source

In 2010, Packt launched two new brands, Packt Open Source and Packt Enterprise, in order to continue its focus on specialization. This book is part of the Packt Open Source brand, home to books published on software built around open source licenses, and offering information to anybody from advanced developers to budding web designers. The Open Source brand also runs Packt's Open Source Royalty Scheme, by which Packt gives a royalty to each open source project about whose software a book is sold.

Writing for Packt

We welcome all inquiries from people who are interested in authoring. Book proposals should be sent to author@packtpub.com. If your book idea is still at an early stage and you would like to discuss it first before writing a formal book proposal, then please contact us; one of our commissioning editors will get in touch with you.

We're not just looking for published authors; if you have strong technical skills but no writing experience, our experienced editors can help you develop a writing career, or simply get some additional reward for your expertise.

open source
community experience distilled

Mastering MariaDB

Mastering MariaDB

Debug, secure, and back up your data for optimum server
performance with MariaDB

Federico Razzoli

Mastering MariaDB

ISBN: 978-1-78398-154-0   Paperback: 384 pages

Debug, secure, and back up your data for optimum
server performance with MariaDB

1. Monitor database activity and the
   major operating system parameters
   to improve performance.

2. Tweak the behaviour of a large number of
   servers to achieve the desired level of stability
   and reliability.

3. Solve the typical problems related to running
   a server, such as slow queries, long locks,
   and so on.

MariaDB Cookbook

MariaDB Cookbook

Over 95 recipes to unlock the power of MariaDB

Daniel Bartholomew

MariaDB Cookbook

ISBN: 978-1-78328-439-9   Paperback: 282 pages

Over 95 recipes to unlock the power of MariaDB

1. Enable performance-enhancing optimizations.

2. Connect to different databases and file formats.

3. Filled with clear step-by-step instructions that
   can be run on a live database.

Please check **www.PacktPub.com** for information on our titles

MariaDB High Performance

ISBN: 978-1-78398-160-1   Paperback: 298 pages

Familiarize yourself with the MariaDB system and build high-performance applications

1. Build multiple slaves and load balance with HA-Proxy.

2. Explore MariaDB 10 features like GTID replication or Sharding using Spider.

3. This is a step-by-step tutorial guide to help you build high performance applications.

Getting Started with MariaDB
Second Edition

ISBN: 978-1-78528-412-0   Paperback: 140 pages

Explore the powerful features of MariaDB with practical examples

1. Install, configure, and manage MariaDB.

2. Store and manipulate data with MariaDB.

3. Get up and running with real-world, practical examples based on MariaDB 10.

Please check **www.PacktPub.com** for information on our titles

Printed in Great
Britain
by Amazon

32058727R00118